RESCUE A

REACHING THE LEAST, LAST, & LOST

GENERATION

JOSE RODRIGUEZ

Publishing Team

Content Editor
Kyle Wiltshire

Director, Student Ministry
Ben Trueblood

Production Editor
Brooke Hill

Manager, Student Ministry Publishing
John Paul Basham

Graphic Designer
Shiloh Stufflebeam

Editorial Team Leader
Karen Daniel

Published by Lifeway Press®
©2022 Jose Rodriguez

ISBN 978-1-0877-5602-8
Item 005835894
Dewey Decimal Classification Number: 230
Subject Heading: RELIGION / CHRISTIAN MINISTRY / YOUTH

Printed in the United States of America

Student Ministry Publishing
Lifeway Resources
One Lifeway Plaza
Nashville, Tennessee 37234

We believe that the Bible has God for its author; salvation for its end; and truth, without any mixture of error, for its matter and that all Scripture is totally true and trustworthy. To review Lifeway's doctrinal guideline, please visit www.lifeway.com/doctrinalguideline.

Contents

About the Author

Jose Rodriguez

Growing up in the inner city, Jose Rodriguez was faced with many of the same challenges students are faced with today. Impacted by his environment, he made some poor choices. He joined a gang, got arrested for stealing cars, and was regularly suspended from school. His story is one that many teens growing up in an urban setting can relate to today, but it's also a story of a complete turnaround.

Jose is the founder and CEO of Rescue a Generation Inc., a non-profit that focuses on reaching students who are struggling in school due to behavior, suspensions, and family issues. He is a sought-out communicator who speaks to students in a variety of venues across the nation. His passion for young people, authenticity, and boldness gives him the tools to effectively help all of us reach and rescue this generation.

Introduction

Have you ever had a student in your ministry who gives you a migraine every time they are around? A type of student that seems as if they are always looking for reasons not to listen or to get in trouble and be rebellious? I'm sure every time you saw this student coming, you were filled with grace and mercy and wished nothing but the Lord's richest blessings toward him or her.

Nah, let's get real. Maybe if some of those students didn't show up, the event might go smoother, other students might be more focused, and you would be able to give attention to the ones who are there for the right reasons, correct?

Have you ever asked why this student is this way? It's possible they are this way because of deep pain in their lives. It's possible their environment has shaped them to act like this. It's possible they are drowning and need rescue. The truth is, these hard-to-reach students need the hope of the gospel just as much as everyone else.

The challenge is that sometimes getting past the walls they put up seems nearly impossible. It seems as if they just won't get it. Is the effort you are putting in worth it? Will you really see the change you are praying for?

I know it is hard. I know it gets frustrating. I know there are moments you just want to give up. But what if you're the only person who won't stop believing in them? In this book, we will dive into how to reach some of the hardest to reach students in your youth group, on your campus, or in your community. Many of them do not need to be reached; they need to be rescued. Let's dive in and see how we can rescue the least, the last, and the lost.

Foreword

In the spring of 2014, I had an opportunity to teach and train a group of emerging urban leaders on a systematic approach to developing an effective and efficient urban ministry program at Biola University in Southern California. This training aimed to provide leaders with some practical tools and strategies that would help them assemble the proper structure to fit their specific cultural context and teach them how to empower the right leaders to fulfill their godly vision and mission. There were so many incredible and gifted leaders in the training who were passionate about reaching the next generation. Little did I know that one of the cohort members would end up having a profound impact on my life. The cohort member I'm referring to was Jose Rodriguez.

At this point, I had served for the past twenty years as a youth pastor and executive pastor in an urban church in Atlanta, Georgia. Although I had the privilege of crossing paths with many exceptional leaders, there was something uniquely different about Jose. While many other youth leaders only talked about reaching the next generation, Jose had a multi-level vision for reaching and rescuing a generation.

Jose and I connected, and I got a chance to hear his story. Now, in an effort not to spoil what you're about to read, all I can say is: when I heard Jose's story, I was blown away. Despite Jose's upbringing, trials, and tribulations, there was such a joy that came over him as he shared his testimony on how his encounter with Jesus changed the trajectory of his life forever! Ever since our first meeting, I have watched Jose spend his life living out the principles of what it means to rescue a generation.

After meeting Jose, two things were clear to me. First, Jose is a gifted leader that God is using in an extraordinary way.

Second, Jose has a deep love, passion, and compassion for marginalized, under-resourced, and overlooked students—students like he was. The least, the last, and the lost. Jose isn't just talking about it, he's being about it!

Some of you picked up this book simply because you thought the title was pretty cool and catchy. However, I promise you, as you read through it, you're going to find that Jose does a masterful job of challenging and inspiring us all. He encourages us not only to join the movement of rescuing a generation, but he will also stretch us to step outside of our comfort zones to become the leaders God has designed us to be. Many people create resources that are one-sided and only discuss the "what," but not many people will deep dive and teach the "why" and the "how." This book will provide a road map that will equip you with the necessary tools to learn how to reach students many people feel are hard to reach or even unreachable.

Jose continues to inspire me to be a better leader. He inspires me to remember that God is still a God who specializes in making the impossible possible! Jose's story may not be your story; however, so many students like Jose need leaders like YOU to accept the challenge of rescuing a generation. No matter where you live or what your student ministry context is, this book will fundamentally equip you with the tools you need to connect with those hard-to-reach students your church is missing.

Jeffrey Wallace
Executive Director of the LIFT Tour & Youth Pastor Summit
Student Leadership University

PART

WHY

Chapter 1
Why Rescue?

I'll never forget my first time on a cruise ship. I was so nervous about everything. I knew that the vast majority of cruise ships made it to their destination and back without a problem, but I couldn't seem to shake the "what if" thoughts. What if we sink? What if there's bad weather? What if there's a medical emergency? I put up a good front the entire way to the ship. I could have won an Oscar for my performance! I acted as if I was only excited and not nervous at all. After all, I was a newlywed and was about to spend a week on a boat with my wife. Truth be told, I was terrified. My thoughts kept drifting back to the worst-case scenarios. It was like Titanic was replaying in my head and my wife and I were Jack and Rose.

Once we boarded, we went to our room to get settled in and then we explored what the boat had to offer. It had restaurants, activities, and even jacuzzis to take it easy in. Finally, I began to relax. My anxiety started to be overtaken by genuine excitement over all the fun we could have together on the ship.

Later that evening, we were summoned to a large room with the passengers on the boat from our same deck. Once we were in the room, they gave us a presentation on the safety protocols for the ship. They described where to go in case of an emergency, what to do if the boat began to sink, and what to do if you had a problem while on one of the day excursions. At this point, my anxiety came rushing back, and my worst-case-scenario thinking took over again. All I kept thinking about was that we were going to the middle of the ocean, so who would make it in time to rescue us if we needed to be saved?

We ended up having the absolute time of our lives as a newlywed couple and thoroughly enjoyed all of the amenities the ship had to offer. Once we made it back to land safely, we had incredible stories to tell from our experience on the cruise. However, the more I reflected on this trip, I discovered a strange parallel to student ministry.

REACHING AND RESCUING

When I was in college studying youth ministry, I learned so many valuable principles about effectively reaching students. I learned not just about students but about reaching their families as well. One particular class taught me the importance of properly communicating with parents as well as students. As I sat in that class, I fully agreed with what was being taught, but I had a tough time applying what I was learning to the situation of the students I was ministering to.

At this time, I served a youth ministry that was considered an urban youth outreach ministry. Each week, we ran eight buses into the inner city of Tulsa, Oklahoma. We would bring in around two hundred to two hundred fifty inner-city students from various neighborhoods in our community. To give you a better context of what this ministry looked like, police and armed security were required at each worship service due to the population of students we were bringing in. They would often bring their drama, gang issues, and drug paraphernalia to church to do what they were doing in their neighborhoods.

On several occasions, we found ourselves in the middle of breaking up fights, both gang-related and just over an offense that happened at church. We had to keep our eyes open from beginning to end to ensure students could manage their emotions and behave appropriately. These were the types of students who have a hard time trusting anybody—especially somebody in authority. That meant if I wanted to reach them effectively, I had to take the time to get to know them in a personal way. They did not care if I was a pastor or not, or if I was in ministry or not—they only cared if I took the time to get to know them.

If I wanted to reach them effectively, I had to take the time to get to know them in a personal way.

Each week, to build rapport with the students on my particular bus, I would go for a few hours into a section eight housing apartment complex to hang out on the basketball court and in their environment. As I began to get to know these students, it was very apparent that they lacked parental guidance and leadership in their lives. These young people were pretty much able to do whatever they wanted to do, whenever they wanted to do it. Unfortunately, most of what they desired to do involved them finding their way into some trouble.

As I spent more and more time with these students, I learned why their parents let them do anything they wanted— they either weren't there or didn't care. It was then I realized these particular students were already bombarded with pain, trauma, and abuse from their households, communities, and peers. They were already drowning in the unstable situations of their homes and everyday lives.

That was when I realized these students did not just need to be reached; they needed to be rescued. They needed to be rescued from pain and trauma. They needed to be rescued from their broken family systems. They needed to be rescued from the toxic gang culture that they so easily bought into. They needed to be rescued by the gospel of Jesus Christ!

Youth ministry is not a safe ministry to serve in. It involves rolling up your sleeves or pant legs and getting in the trenches with students. It requires us to do things like Jesus did—leave our comfort zones and live among the people. It's messy and chaotic, but also fulfilling when you realize you are answering the call of reaching and rescuing a generation. It's kind of like my cruise experience. If I was only afraid of what could happen and I gave into my anxiety, emotions, and fear, I would have missed the reward and joy of being on a memorable trip with my wife. Ministry is messy, but the reward of seeing students turn away from their old lives and follow the life that Jesus has for them is one of the most rewarding feelings you can experience in life and ministry.

LIFEBOAT

Every cruise ship has a lifeboat. You hope to never be in one, but you're glad they are there if they are needed. It's the idea of the lifeboat that I would like to present as a paradigm for ministry to urban and at-risk students today. Youth ministry has evolved over the last few decades. Students today are dealing with so much more fear and anxiety than in the past. In many ways, youth ministry in the 90s was different—safer. Overall, the church had a reputation as a safe place. It was a place students knew they could go when their lives got chaotic. It was regarded as a lifeboat, or a place where a student could go to be safe.

When I was in college, I heard an alarming prediction. Ron Luce, founder of Acquire the Fire, said that if something did not change, only 4 percent of the next generation would be Bible-believing Christians.[1] I heard this in 2007. I am not sure people realized how prophetic that statement was. In 2018, the Barna group came out with a study about Gen Z and Millennials that said only 6 percent of Millennials and only 4 percent of Gen Z are Bible-believing Christians.[2]

This is where my heart is and is the framework for my whole ministry. I believe that Jesus is the way, the truth, and the life, and no one comes to God apart from Him (see John 14:6). I also believe Luke 5:31-32, where Jesus said He did not come for the healthy but for the sick. Therefore, the local church is designed to be a lifeboat to rescue the drowning. Since both of these understandings reflect our responsibility as believers, that means only 6 percent of Millennials and 4 percent of Gen Z are safely in the boat. However, 96 percent of Gen Z students are drowning in a world of pain, trauma, depression, anxiety, suicide, fatherlessness, drugs, and so much more. We can no longer be comfortable just trying to keep safe the 4 percent in the boat. Our responsibility as youth workers is to go after the millions of other students in this generation dying from their issues. There is a generation drowning that needs to be rescued.

MY JOURNEY

At the end of my time in college, I just knew God was going to open up big doors for me at some megachurch and be a radical youth pastor who reached hundreds of students overnight. Instead, God had different plans for me. He sent me to San Bernardino, California.

I'll never forget moving into a new city full of ambition, hope, and Jesus. I just knew God would use me to grow our youth ministry from twenty students to hundreds within months. After all, that is what God sent me to the city to do, right? However, in 2012, the city of San Bernardino filed for bankruptcy. At the time, it was the largest city of its kind to file for bankruptcy and the second poorest large city in the nation, second only to Detroit. I knew I had the gifts, the skill set, and the passion for reaching this generation. I got to my new home and was handed the keys to the youth ministry to run with it full-time. I began to take all of my knowledge from serving inner-city students for the previous ten years and the things I learned in college. It was now time to live it out.

It was not long before I realized the training I received, while essential and necessary, didn't quite apply to the students I was serving. I realized that for me to impact their lives, I would need to show up for them. Showing up did not necessarily look like going to their basketball games or track meets. These were the type of situations that I was used to. Showing up for these kids looked like being in the courtroom so the student knew I was with them and God still had a plan for them despite whatever crime they had committed.

These students have given me my fair share of courtroom experiences, hospital visits, and even police encounters. No matter where serving them takes me, I am committed to them until the end. No matter the cost, the crime, or the situation, I will be there to make sure they know they are not alone and can be rescued at any moment. If I'm being honest, I've had quite a few frustrating moments—the types of moments that make me want to quit and walk away from the very thing that God has called me to do. It is in those moments that I—and you, too, if you want to serve students like this—must remember the "why" and find small victories to celebrate so the feeling of failure doesn't become overwhelming. Remember, our responsibility is to be obedient to what God has called us to do. If you will be faithful to that, then you can trust Him with the results.

> **Ultimately, the only reason I'm writing this is because God, in all of His sovereignty, saw fit to rescue a little, broken, Hispanic boy from the inner city of Tulsa, Oklahoma.**

RESCUE?

I am fully aware that on my best day, I cannot rescue anyone. Ultimately, it is by the grace of God that any of us find ourselves saved. However, God has always had an answer for the issues that have plagued our society. From Genesis to Revelation, God has always had a response for every problem we've faced. He has used people to bring about His plans, will, and desires.

Consider the Hebrews, trapped in slavery and oppression. God raised up Moses to be the answer and a deliverer of an entire generation. If you look at the rebellion of all humankind and God's grief at even creating humans in the first place, God raised up Noah to build an ark and save his family, saving all of humanity. If you look at the corrupt leadership of a country that was supposed to be His chosen people, God raised a man after His own heart—David. If you factor in a church with issues and perversion among believers, God raised up Paul to be a missionary and to write letters to bring correction to the house of God. If you factor in all of humanity's sin and the rebellion and fall of humanity, God sent Himself in the person of Jesus to pay the ultimate sacrifice so that we all should not perish but have everlasting life if we believe in Him. God is never without an answer to the pains of a generation, and He uses people to help in the rescue that only He is able to achieve.

Ultimately, the only reason I'm writing this is because God, in all of His sovereignty, saw fit to rescue a little, broken, Hispanic boy from the inner city of Tulsa, Oklahoma. A boy who was already drowning in a world of trauma, sin, and poverty. Jesus never came out of the sky to appear to me. Instead, He would raise up a lady named Nancy who would knock on my door over and over and over again to invite me to church.

If God never raised up Nancy, I have no idea where I would be today. I know that God is still empowering and using people around the world. The whole reason you have this book now is probably because there is a burden in your heart for this generation that God has placed inside of you. You are not satisfied with the 4 percent in the boat. You know He wants to use you to get in the trenches with this generation so we can see God raise up youth workers to be rescuers of students in every neighborhood, every demographic, and every socio-economic status. There is a generation that needs the rescuing only God can offer. I am convinced if you have been in youth ministry for longer than five minutes, you know it is not going to be an easy job. It will involve you getting messy as you do life with students who need the hope of the gospel.

As we work through the rest of this book, I pray you, as the rescuer God can use, find hope, resourceful ideas, and motivation to continue to fight for this generation. They don't just need you; they need God. I believe that together, with the power of the Holy Spirit, we can and we will rescue this generation.

Chapter 1 Reflection Questions

1. What are some of the ways students you work with need to be rescued and not just reached?

2. How have you seen ministry change since you've started in student ministry?

3. In what ways have you had to go beyond your standard programming to help students who are struggling?

Scan the QR code for teaching videos from author Jose Rodriguez.

RESCUE A GENERATION

Chapter 2
Why Urban?

Have you ever walked into a room and immediately stood out as different from everyone else? Like the type of standing out that makes you feel uncomfortable or awkward even being there? Maybe you went to a party and were the only person in a costume. Or maybe on the first day of school, you had a wardrobe malfunction that was so noticeable you knew something had to change for you to make it through the day. If any of these scenarios resonate with you, I believe you'll be able to understand the heart behind this chapter.

In our fast-growing, urban world, we see more and more issues and conversations around racial reconciliation, gender equality, and the fight for an equal opportunity no matter where a person comes from. While I believe that many of those conversations are absolutely necessary and, to an extent, long overdue, that is not entirely the focus of this conversation. In fact, focusing on one aspect of these issues would minimize the heart behind this more significant concern—not being understood.

DIFFERENT

Growing up in the middle of an inner-city, I realized that there were things about my neighborhood, environment, and the people closest to me that were different from what I would eventually see in the rest of the world. I was not aware enough at the time to recognize all the intricacies that would come with being considered "urban." However, I did know that my experience was different.

When I came to faith, it became so much more evident that there was something utterly different about my experience growing up. When I started going to church, I would go on a Saturday because that was when the bus ministry for the megachurch I attended came and picked me up. The kids that would come to church through the bus ministry all looked and sounded like me—not necessarily in race but in culture. The people who would pick us up on the buses—the leaders, bus captains, and preachers—all looked completely different than me. I knew then that there was a difference between those of us who were being reached and the ones who were trying to reach us.

That difference became magnified even more when I was introduced to the church on a day other than Saturday and in a way other than the bus ministry. My mentor, Nancy, who I briefly mentioned in the last chapter, started to take a group of us "Leaders in Training" to church on Sunday morning. It was a unique yet challenging experience for me.

Imagine that costume party I mentioned earlier. That is what going to church felt like every Sunday for me. I would show up in my regular clothes because I did not have other clothes to wear. My usual outfit was a long baggy t-shirt and some oversized jeans. My clothes were probably dirty and dingy because we did not have a washer and dryer in our home, so having clean clothes regularly was challenging. I was a super skinny Latino boy who had extremely curly hair I barely cared for. I smelled of cigarette smoke each week because both of my parents were smokers.

I remember the first time going to church at the large, charismatic megachurch known for its outreach programs for the lost, particularly in low-income communities. I was so excited to go to the bigger church that weekend with a few of my friends so I would actually got to see what church for adults was really like. Six of us were going for the first time that Sunday morning. All six of us crammed into a super small Honda Civic because we wanted to go that badly. We probably did not follow every traffic law to get us there, but thank God we got there in one piece. If you've ever done youth ministry in a context where you had to pick up students to get them to church, there may have been times when you needed to be pretty creative to get everyone there.

I knew then that there was a difference between those of us who were being reached and the ones who were trying to reach us.

We finally got across town and piled out of the car one by one, ready to ascend the immaculate escalators to the sanctuary. People were walking in with their families, nicely dressed and smiling as if they had the most fantastic ride to church. Then there was us—a group of teens without our families and looking terribly out of place. People could have assumed that we were there to cause some sort of disruption, and quite honestly, we probably did, but not intentionally. We just didn't know any better.

By the time we got to the top of the escalator, greeters had said hello to us from the parking lot to the sanctuary. Most of these greeters were smiling from ear to ear and welcomed us in the warmest way possible—until we got to the top. Just as we were getting ready to enter the foyer, there was a greeter passing out bulletins for the church. I stood in line, ready to receive my bulletin when the guy at the door looked at me and handed the bulletin to the person behind me. In his defense, I was a teen. I truly wasn't that interested, but I was just trying to do what I thought I was supposed to do.

Now, I am not trying to make more of this situation than I should. I am very aware that this could have just been the luck that I walked into. However, it was the first situation that day that made me feel like I was not important enough to be there. As we entered the sanctuary, some people looked and smiled. Others looked as if we were the only ones in costume at the party. I remember leaving that day feeling in some ways that I did not belong. As I recalled this situation, I realized this would become the first of many similar circumstances in which I would feel like I was the outcast in the faith community—like I wasn't understood.

I UNDERSTAND

In this book, we will explore how to reach some of the hard-to-reach students in and around our ministries. A question that needs to be answered is, "What makes these students hard to reach?" I am not a therapist and I do not have a degree in psychology, but I have spent all of my life in low-income communities as a student and then as a youth worker trying to reach and rescue this generation. What I have found repeatedly is that many people mean well when they try to reach urban students, but they tend to lack the one thing that will help them connect: understanding. You can learn principles and have the heart for students, but if you do not understand where they are coming from and why they are acting the way they act, then you will lack the empathy and ability to truly help them move past their own brokenness.

In my second year in Bible college, we had to do a project in an evangelism class. It consisted of identifying a group of people to do some research and interviews with in order to gain a better understanding of the people and their lives. I was excited that we were assigned this project because, for me, the choice of people was easy. I was going to target gang members because I came out of that lifestyle and had easy access to people we could set up interviews with. I'll share more about this in the next chapter.

I was able to gather a group of fellow Bible college students from diverse backgrounds who were willing to do the project and interview gang members with me. We spent time doing research on gang activities and the history of gangs. For some reason, they all assumed gang members were all terribly evil people. I was almost offended as we began conversations because I used to be one of these guys, and I didn't see myself that way. I knew most people like myself turned to gangs as a means of survival. My environment affected every decision I made. There is a reason these environments are called "The Trap." It's called that because people don't make it out. This is why it's so hard to reach students who live in these communities.

You can learn principles and have the heart for students, but if you do not understand where they are coming from and why they are acting the way they act, then you will lack the empathy and ability to truly help them move past their own brokenness.

As we dove deeper into the project, it was finally time to interview people in the gang. The guys from the gang that I knew would be at a house where, frankly, illegal things would be taking place. We had to iron out the details about what would and wouldn't be covered in the project and that the Bible college students wouldn't report what they saw to the police.

Finally, an agreement was reached and the interviews could be conducted.

As we got to the house, there were around fifteen people hanging out. They were all wearing the same colors. They were drinking and smoking weed and there were other people who would come pick up drugs and drive off. As each side observed the other and what was happening, I was able to gather everybody in a circle so we could ask our interview questions and get the assignment done.

Things were going great, and both groups seemed to be getting along pretty well even though it was like a mixture of oil and water coming together. In the middle of the conversation, the guy whose house we were at came out with a machine gun, laughing and yelling, "This is how we do things around here!"

The looks on the faces of the people from the Bible college were priceless, even though it was a scary situation. One of the guys from the Bible college broke the stunned silence, looked at the guy with the gun, and said the worst thing anyone could in a situation like that: "I understand."

I was so frustrated. I knew there was no way he really understood what was happening beyond what he saw. He sure did not understand why it was happening. It's detrimental to say "I understand" when you really have absolutely no way of understanding. If you really want to understand, you have to do the work to learn about the what and the why for the students you are trying to reach.

We were able to finish the interviews and get the project done, but I will never forget what it was like combining those two worlds and worldviews at once. I was in the middle and was probably the only one who understood both sides of the circle. I knew the man meant well, but you don't just understand people because you've seen them one time. Understanding takes real work and time to get a grasp on the people you are trying to understand. For many, it takes years.

POVERTY

There are urban students around the world that we, as believers, have missed because it has been hard to identify or relate to students from diverse backgrounds. Thank God for Nancy. Nancy and I had little to nothing in common. In fact, our stories, backgrounds, and upbringings were not even close. However, Nancy knew that you do not have to be relevant to reach. Nancy invested in me for so long that I allowed her into my space and I began to trust that she was genuinely concerned for me. Nancy loved me beyond the walls of brokenness that I put up.

Urban students have walls up for a variety of reasons. One of the primary issues many urban students face today is the issue of poverty. Poverty comes across mainly in conversations as an economic issue. However, the issue of poverty affects so many other areas than a person's money. In her book, *A Framework to Understanding Poverty*, Dr. Ruby Payne laid out eight different types of poverty. The definition she provides for poverty is "the extent to which one does not have the resources."[3] These eight poverty types are spiritual poverty, intellectual poverty, poverty of affection, poverty of the will, poverty of solidarity, physical poverty, economic poverty, and poverty of civic engagement. These poverty types ultimately make up a significant portion of what we see in students from urban communities and are a major contributing factor in how students behave. They are also subjective to the individual. Some students may struggle with one of these and not the others.

While the world is growing more urban, looking at poverty through this lens means that it is not exclusive to urban students. Suburban students may not deal with the same types of poverty, but they struggle with poverty as well. We are seeing the effects of poverty on students around the world.

We could spend time breaking down each of these, but I would like to highlight a few that directly affect students we are trying to reach.

SPIRITUAL POVERTY

Spiritual poverty might seem a little obvious, but think back to my experience. I had a chance to come out of spiritual poverty, but my first real opportunity was hindered by my own perception of the people in the church and their perception of me. Efforts to end my own spiritual poverty could have been hindered because I did not feel understood by the people trying to reach me.

Ultimately, there is not a one-size-fits-all approach to ending spiritual poverty for all people. We have to go about reaching some completely differently from others. If the goal is to help students have the resources and ability to grow and develop spiritually, our number one responsibility is to make sure they feel loved and accepted enough to belong so they can eventually grow in their spiritual life.

Every person needs to hear the gospel, but there is no such thing as a quick fix. When we venture into low-income communities or to third-world countries to preach the gospel, we must take care to not notch our own gospel belt. We cannot seek to work in spiritually poverty-stricken areas expecting a quick solution. If there was a quick solution, then spiritual poverty would no longer exist.

We must understand that to be effective, we have to be in it for the long haul. Spiritual poverty is not irradicated in a moment but rather through a process in which a person's mind, body, heart, and soul are renewed and restored. More often than not, this happens through a discipleship relationship; a person who comes alongside another who helps them grow out of the trappings of spiritual poverty.

POVERTY OF AFFECTION

Broken homes and fatherlessness have a massive effect on students today. These issues don't just affect them now but as they grow into adulthood as well. The implications of the fatherless epidemic in our country has less to do with the fathers and mother and more to do with the sons and daughters. The statistics of students in fatherless homes are alarming. Consider the following statistics:

+ Young boys living without fathers are more likely to be the cause of male juvenile violent crimes.[4]

+ Fatherless sons are at a dramatically greater risk of criminality, fathering children as teenagers, subpar educational performance, suicide, mental illness, and drug and alcohol abuse. Daughters of single parents without fathers involved are 53 percent more likely to marry as teenagers, 711 percent more likely to have children as teenagers, 164 percent more likely to have a premarital birth, and 92 percent more likely to get divorced themselves.[5]

+ Sixty-three percent of youth suicides are children from fatherless homes; five times the national average. Ninety percent of homeless runaway children are from fatherless homes; 32 times the national average.[6]

+ Youth violence has become a national public health emergency. Youth ages ten to twenty-five years commit almost 50 percent of crimes. Twenty-one percent of all sixteen-year-olds arrested have already been arrested by twelve years of age.[7]

The poverty of affection is a direct result of broken families. In some cases, this does not mean the absent dad has left the mom or was never present to begin with. It could mean, like in my case, the dad was missing because he worked hard to provide but was not there emotionally for his children. Either way, the effects are the same. Children need affection, and when it's not present, the result is poverty of affection. This leads to so many damaging relationships, and young people explore ways to find affection from whoever will give it.

In inner cities, many young men and women will find that level of affection in the gangs in their neighborhoods. Gangs have become the replacement family so many are looking for. If students did not struggle with poverty of affection, we would not see gangs grow at the rate they do. Gangs become the source of affirmation, acceptance, and love for so many urban students. Students commit to gangs because they feel like the gangs commit to them. We then see the aftermath of that loyalty in the result of crimes, bad behavior, and illegal activities.

Poverty of affection is not just limited to financially poor communities. We see young people in wealthy communities who find themselves on drugs because of the lack of love in their families. Students are looking for a way to either replace the affection or numb the pain from the lack of love shown regularly. Humans were created with the need for affection. When we do not get it, we find ourselves at a higher risk of finding that in an unhealthy way or place.

POVERTY OF SOLIDARITY

Poverty of solidarity is the lack of support shown in the lives of individuals. This poverty directly affects those who are in low-income communities and people who grew up in the inner city. One of the many reasons why growing up in these environments can be so damaging is the lack of support and lack of knowledge. This does not mean that there is no support available; it simply means people are not educated enough to know what support is available to them.

One of the critical factors in students who overcome the odds in their lives is whether they have people in solidarity with them. We have all heard the phrase "it takes a village to raise a child." It means the child was not alone. There were organizations, sports teams, mentors, or other places of support that ultimately helped them get to the place where they could beat the odds.

This poverty affected my family tremendously as I was growing up. The only level of solidarity we had came from each other. You would think this would be good, but when solidarity comes from people stuck on drugs, welfare, and gangs, nobody is really helping anybody get better.

After I gave my life to Christ, I decided that I would go to a Christian school in order to change my environment and be around other students who were pursuing their relationship with God. One of the most frustrating things for me being at that school was how I witnessed other families show up for their students. I felt like I was by myself.

This followed me all the way to college. I'll never forget being accepted into Oral Roberts University and preparing to get enrolled. I reached out to my mom and told her we needed to register for my classes. My mom's response was honest, but it reflected the lack of solidarity in my family. My mom told me she did not know what to do to get me registered because she had never been to college. I remember feeling once again like I had to fend for myself. Many young people in urban America are foregoing pursuing higher education simply because they lack solidarity with the right people who can help advocate for them and gain access to schools and opportunities.

URBAN

The use of the word urban can be directly correlated with some aspects of the word poverty. Jeff Wallace and Lenieta Fix define the word urban in their book, *Everybody's Urban,* as, "any student, from any race, religion, culture, or style, who merely exists to survive the day."[8]

Urban is survival. When a person is constantly living in survival mode day to day, they would be considered urban. Urban is no longer only confined to ghettos in the inner city of America, though it is still very much the culture of those communities. Now, we are seeing the spread of what urban culture has created in this generation. Under this definition, urban can be the students in the rural community struggling with drugs and feeling hopeless. It could also be students in wealthy communities feeling unloved and struggling with depression, anxiety, and suicidal ideations. Urban is no longer identified by race or location. Urban is the world we live in.

In the world we live in today, we must not just exegete the text but learn to exegete the people.

I was invited to speak at a camp in Michigan to a group of students that I thought was far from an urban context. As I got to the camp and spent a few days with the students, it was apparent that the line was not as clear as I first thought. Some of those students were in just as much of a survival mode as the students I ministered to in San Bernardino. Their survival was in a different context, but it was still survival.

It is not just poverty and pain that connects this urban generation; it is also very much the urban influence on pop culture that is prevalent. Urban culture has grown drastically since social media has taken over students' lives. However, I do believe there is a clear difference between urban culture and the urban experience. For instance, the Kardashians would be considered urban culture. They have played a big part in this generation, as we've watched them live, grow up, and glamorize urban culture. But I do not think that the Kardashians have had an urban experience, meaning living and growing up in adverse environments, constantly fighting for survival, and being labeled as at-risk or high-risk.

Today, students consume and have access to almost the same media no matter who they are or where they are from. This has caused the line of being urban to be more blurred than ever before.

WHAT DOES THIS MEAN FOR US?

As believers, leaders, youth workers, and people who want to see this generation won for Christ, we must learn the culture we are trying to engage. I am not asking you to listen to secular music all day to stay relevant to your students because I do not think you need to be relevant to reach. However, I am saying that the world we live in looks completely different from when some of us came to faith. We now have a responsibility to engage this different world that we live in.

If you have had any ministry training, you have probably learned aspects of hermeneutics and how to exegete the Scriptures. Being a student of the Bible keeps you from being heretical. It allows you to know the context and see things from the perspective of the writer of the text. I have seen so many modern-day theologians be experts at the Word but not experts of the times or the people. In the world we live in today, we must not just exegete the text but learn to exegete the people. Be a constant learner of the urban world we live in. Learn the pains, struggles, survival methods, and coping mechanisms of the students we are trying to reach.

As we commit to learning more and more about this world we live in and the pains of the people God calls us to reach, we must not be afraid to get close to them. When I came to faith and began going to church, you would be surprised at how many people seemed afraid of getting close to me. It was almost as if I had some form of leprosy. Urban students do not have leprosy. They desperately need somebody to see beyond their struggles and get close enough to show them Jesus. We cannot effectively reach this urban world from a distance. It will require us to get close enough to touch them, eat with them, and ask them questions.

Whether we know it or not or embrace it or not, the world is still becoming more urban. Don't let the word "urban" distract you. Students each of us seeks to reach may not look urban but are constantly in survival mode internally. Our commitment to learning this generation and getting close to young people despite their walls and struggles will ultimately enable us to make disciples of an urban nation.

Chapter 2 Reflection Questions

1. What types of poverty have you seen in the community you are ministering in?

2. How have you seen poverty affect the students you work with?

3. How does this shape how you reach students who are struggling with these issues?

 Scan the QR code for teaching videos from author Jose Rodriguez.

Chapter 3

Why Me?

Do you remember that story in the Bible about the guy who spent his life persecuting and hunting down anybody who was a follower of Jesus? In one moment's time, everything changed for him. In Acts 9:3, a light from heaven blinded him and Jesus confronted him about his persecuting ways. This began a process of transformation where he shifted from Saul, the terrorizer of the church, to Paul, the apostle to the Gentiles. Even after his transformation, his reputation still preceded him. There were moments when others were afraid of him simply because of his past. His story is dramatic and powerful and proves there are moments when a person's past continues to impact and shape their future. Paul gives me hope.

> **Every young person wants to belong to a place, space, group, or family.**

This chapter is my full story. I'm sharing my story with you so you can see what God can do in the life of an urban student, but also how challenging it is to reach students like me.

A PLACE TO BELONG

For as long as I can remember, my life has been marked by confusion. Not just because of the chaotic upbringing that I grew up in but also in my racial makeup. I grew up in a poverty-stricken, inner-city environment, predominantly made up of Black and brown people. The problem is, though I grew up in and around them, for most of my life, I never completely belonged to any of these groups. I wasn't enough of any color to be fully accepted by any of their cultures. I am by blood, Native American, White, and Mexican. On top of that, I grew up about a mile away from the site of the Tulsa Race Massacre in a neighborhood known as the Greenwood District. This is a historic, predominantly Black neighborhood. This district was known back in the 1920s as Black Wall Street. It was an area where African-American businesses thrived. The Tulsa Race Massacre happened because of Jim Crow laws, jealousy, white supremacy, and land lust, all leading up to the destruction and loss of life on May 31 and June 1, 1921.[9]

This is important because growing up in a predominantly Black neighborhood resulted in my trying to mesh with their culture, ways of thinking, and experiences. But I wasn't Black, so I was never fully embraced by them. This was my experience at every turn. I was Mexican but did not speak Spanish. My family only used Spanish to keep drug-related secrets from the kids. I was Native American and was born in a Native American hospital, but outside of the few Pow Wows that I attended, I knew nothing about that side of my heritage. I was also White, but I never fully embraced that side of me because of the places I grew up in. By the age of eleven, I found myself working extra hard to fit in with whichever group I was around the most.

I am not trying to make this all about race. However, I do think race plays a large part in why this book even exists. Every young person wants to belong to a place, space, group, or family. When your childhood lacks a sense of belonging, you go to great lengths to make sure you fit in somewhere with somebody.

For me, this became evident when I was in the sixth grade. We had just moved into the Greenwood District. By this point, I had already become close friends with several of the kids in my neighborhood. This particular neighborhood was run by a gang called the Neighborhood Crips. This was a predominantly Black gang, and all my friends were affiliated with the gang, mainly because of their older siblings. I knew that a big part of my survival in this area was contingent upon my getting along with this gang.

I began to wear the colors, use the language, and even learn the signs of the gang to make sure I fully understood the place where I was living. Truthfully, I only learned these things because I knew if I did not belong to this group, then I would find myself in a world of trouble, and I wanted no part of that. It was a "you're either for us or against us" scenario. I did everything except join the gang. For some reason, I knew that it wasn't the best idea, but I had to be close enough for them to not be against me.

All of that changed one day in the sixth grade after a quiet bus ride home. The bus pulled up to the stop as I noticed our car waiting. Typically, my mom would pick me up from the bus stop and take me home. Everything seemed normal until I got off the bus. I'll never forget the look on my mom's face as I walked to the car. She had tears streaming down her face. It was clear that something was not okay. Earlier that day, my dad had a court date for a driving under the

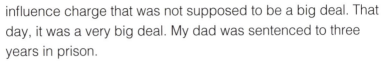

influence charge that was not supposed to be a big deal. That day, it was a very big deal. My dad was sentenced to three years in prison.

The eleven-year-old in me was so broken that my dad would not be around for the next three years. The "man" in me knew that I would need to be the protector for my family. This is almost humorous if you knew how scrawny I was. Nevertheless, I knew I needed to step up to the plate and find a way to survive.

The first couple of weeks were not that bad. Things with my mom, sister, and me functioned normally. Shortly after, we had an incident where somebody approached our house in the middle of the night banging on the door trying to get in. I will never forget the fear in my mom and my sister's voices that night. It was clear to me that we needed protection, and I knew exactly where to get it.

That night, I made the conscious decision to join the gang. I knew they would be like a family to me. I knew they would have my back and that I would feel safe in the neighborhood with their backing. What I did not know was that this decision would lead me down a path that was a lot more dangerous than safe. In that moment, all that mattered was that I finally found a people, a tribe, a community in which I belonged. That changed everything for me. I was willing to do whatever it took for me to remain committed and connected with this group.

ME, AT CHURCH?

It was shortly after I joined this gang that I began to be invited to church on a weekly basis. Every Friday, it was like clockwork. The same person would knock on my door or stop me outside and invite me to join them. He knew I was not interested in going or hearing what he had to say. Every single week, that never stopped him. There is a lesson in this for a later time in this book, but just remember he came by every week, even when I was not even relatively interested.

One day, I was outside playing basketball and I heard the church bus drive down my street. I heard so much laughter, joy, and fun. When the bus stopped a few houses down and let some kids out, I saw everybody had a slice of pizza in their hands. If they had girls and pizza, I was going to church the next time he asked!

The day I first got on the bus, my guard was up. I didn't trust anybody—the kids or the workers. Eventually, I found some friends. We started looking for trouble, which wasn't hard to find, considering this ministry bussed in almost two thousand students every week. For whatever reason, whether it was my defenses being on high alert or just the environment, I was in a rowdy mood that first experience at church. On the bus ride home, it all came to a head.

The bus captain was not quite sure how to handle students like me and my friends. In his defense, we were quite a handful. When we arrived at my stop, he asked me to exit the bus, and he was happy to see me go.

> **It is ultimately heart transformation that leads to the best form of behavior modification.**

The problem was that my sister was going to stay on to help pass out pizza. I told the bus captain that I wasn't leaving the bus until she did. This didn't sit well with him. Without warning or question, he began attempting to pray for me. I did not know what he was doing at the time, but now I know he was reaching his hand to lay it on my head and pray that I would listen and comply. Unfortunately, in that moment, unwanted prayer was not what I needed. I needed him to understand me. I needed him to meet me where I was and not just demand that I comply with his requests.

As soon as his hand was on my head, I reacted the only way I knew how at that point in my life—I laid my hand back on him in the form of a balled-up fist. I got into a fight with my bus captain! Looking back at this moment now is embarrassing.

However, I do think there are some powerful lessons I learned from this moment concerning how we reach and approach at-risk students.

Reflecting on this moment has taught me how hard it is to reach somebody you do not understand. It wasn't his desire to pray for me that led me to throw the first punch. It was the misunderstanding of why I wanted to stay on the bus with my sister. It was me doing the only thing I knew to do when someone puts their hands on you and him automatically expecting me to comply because he said so. It was him thinking my behavior would change through one prayer.

I have learned over the years that behavior modification is never a complete form of change. It is ultimately heart transformation that leads to the best form of behavior modification. If we spend most of our time trying to simply modify a student's behavior in the heat of a moment, we will miss capturing the heart of that student and allowing the gospel to do the changing. In that moment I needed to be understood. I needed to be heard. I needed to be validated. It was a misunderstanding—both his and mine— that created complete chaos that day.

Now, what happens once a student is understood, validated, and belongs to the group? Does that mean the negative behavior stops completely? Not always.

WORSE AND WORSE

After a month's suspension, I was able to come back to the church. I heard about a leadership-in-training (LIT) program the church offered and was interested. What intrigued me wasn't the leadership development or the God stuff. It was the special trips and fun things they did that made me want to join.

Regardless of my motivation, I joined LIT. This put me in a very interesting place. On one hand, I was in a gang and becoming more and more immersed in gang life and culture.

On the other hand, I was showing up at church and joining LIT because I thought it was going to be fun. While I was at church, I was helping on the bus, passing out food, and doing what I could to help people. When I wasn't at church, I was smoking weed and stealing things, starting with candy and eventually growing into much bigger things.

During my freshman year of high school, I played on the basketball team. One day after practice, a teammate said he would drive me home. As a high school student, I didn't ask any questions; I was just excited I had a ride home that wasn't the bus. As we got into the car, I noticed him starting it with a screwdriver. Most teenagers would see something like this, sense something is off, and abort right away. Unfortunately, that was not my story. I observed how he started the car and became intrigued.

On that day, along with a few other "friends," I began a three-month journey of taking cars for joyrides and returning them before we got caught. We did this again and again until we did get caught. Here I was, a fourteen-year-old boy arrested for stealing cars while trying to get involved in church. Once the church found out I was arrested, I thought they would dismiss me or at least asked me to not be in LIT anymore. In fact, the opposite was true. When I had my court date, there was Nancy, the woman who would become my mentor, there just to be with me.

It wasn't until later when I was a youth pastor and had to do the same thing with several of my students that I knew the impact showing up really makes. I've told myself quite often that you know you're an urban youth pastor when you're supporting your students in the courtroom and not on the basketball court. Thank God that Nancy showed me this first.

ME, ON A MISSION TRIP?

I received a deferred sentence that day, which meant if I followed the rules they gave me, I would get off the hook and this incident would not be on my record. During my time on probation, I really began to lean into the LIT program. I knew if I messed up again, I would be in a world of trouble. It was not too long after this court date that I heard about the opportunity to go on a mission trip to Belize.

Initially, I thought there was no way I could go on the trip. I did not have the resources, plus I was on probation. Surely, they wouldn't let me leave the country. Thankfully, I was released from probation just a few weeks prior to the trip, and the leadership of LIT worked extremely hard to raise the money to take twenty-three inner-city students on the trip. I was able to go!

As we prepared for the trip, the church taught me how to tell my story about Jesus saving my life. Everyone on that trip had to write out their one-page testimony. The only problem with my testimony was that I did not believe yet. There was no point prior to that moment when I had fully put my trust in Jesus. I may have said the sinner's prayer, but I didn't really believe. We know according to Romans 10:9 that confession without belief is incomplete. Though I may have confessed to knowing God, I never fully believed in Him.

We got to Belize and began doing ministry at the different schools and communities. We performed "human videos" in large school assemblies. To

As a teenager, I lived the opposite of Hebrews 11:25. Unlike Moses, I chose to live in the pleasures of sin for a season.

my surprise, they asked me to get up and close out the presentation with an altar call. I remember as I was sharing my "testimony," most of my story was extremely real, except for the faith in Christ part. I was talking through the translator (yes, I needed a translator in Spanish), and I asked if the students wanted to receive Jesus as their Lord and Savior. I was shocked. Almost every hand in the building shot up! Here lies the dilemma: these students just put their faith in Christ partly because of the testimony that I shared, and my story was partially a lie. I had just helped hundreds of students put their faith in a Savior that I did not really, fully believe in.

A few nights later, I would have my real salvation moment. On this night, I knew God was real and that I wanted to follow Him for the rest of my life. I completely surrendered to God and said yes to His plan for me. This night changed everything for me, or so I thought.

After coming home, I thought, "I am walking away from everything that is not like God." I decided I was leaving the drugs, the gangs, and the fighting. I was willing to let it all go. Once I got back home, my heart was set on never going back. My family immediately saw something different in me. My sister told me that whatever got into me, she wanted it too. My parents saw a change in me. Everything on the outside looked like I was turning over a new leaf.

PAIN AFTER SALVATION

It didn't take long for me to realize that life still happens after salvation. Nobody warned me that salvation didn't guarantee an easy life. I didn't see the pain coming that I faced just a few weeks after I gave my life to Christ. I did not know how to properly process pain after salvation. I thought Jesus was just going to take it away and make it not happen. I did not realize my yes to God would make me a target for the enemy. Man, he threw a lot at me after I got home.

Shortly after, a couple of my family members were incarcerated, and I did not know how to process this knowledge with my newfound faith in Christ. Unfortunately, I went back to how I coped with pain prior to the trip, which was with marijuana and going back to the gang life. This time, I tried to live in the duality of two worlds, thinking I could keep the two separate. I went to church, served, worshiped, helped, and even transferred to a Christian school, thinking that would change everything for me. But I also still lived in the same neighborhood and had access to all my old friends. I continued to live the life I was living prior to Jesus. The most unique part about it all was that I felt like I was good at living a double life—until my old ways crept into my new life.

A CHURCH VAN?

Even though I joined a couple of friends from the LIT program at a Christian school, not every student at that Christian school was interested in going after God. It was even worse for me, being from the inner city and resembling what many of my new classmates had been seeing on TV. It was not long until we were all caught up in the wrong crowd. I found myself suspended on more than one occasion for drugs, fighting, and other reasons. I had a very hard time succeeding in this new environment. So much of what I had been taught up to that point in my life was contrary to the standards of this new school. For instance, I was suspended for having a condom in my possession. This was so shocking to me because I was taught by public schools my whole life to practice safe sex, yet I was told that having a condom was wrong once I got to this new school.

The biggest thing that happened to me while I was in this school was realizing that I really had not known full repentance and I still had a desire to do what I knew was wrong. In part, I needed to renew my mind and change the understandings I had been taught my entire life. At the same time, there were still parts of me that were there just because I was rebellious and struggled with the excitement that sin and crime brought me. As a teenager, I lived the opposite of Hebrews 11:25. Unlike Moses, I chose to live in the pleasures of sin for a season. Sin was enticing, attractive, exhilarating, and destructive. I found myself choosing that over God over and over again.

Then the rubber hit the road—literally. My friends and I could never afford to go to the school even with the discounts we were given. For us to pay our way through the school, we had to join the event staff at the church and work for our tuition. Unfortunately, our old ways of life still led us down wrong roads we were all too willing to walk. As we were working, or supposed to be working, we made the decision to clock in and ditch work. We decided to grab the keys to the church van and take it for a joy ride. That first day we did not go far because we were terrified. However, getting away with it opened up a new desire to do this more often.

For about a month, on a weekly basis, we took the keys, and as fifteen-year-olds, would drive the van around the city, hoping nobody would notice. It seemed the more we got away with it, the riskier we became. We started smoking weed in the vans and driving around places that were easier for people to spot us. This was not just a plain white van; it had the name of the church plastered on the side of the window. We are talking about a fifteen-thousand-member megachurch. To think we were getting away with this was almost as foolish as doing it in the first place.

One day, I was all alone at work. We had a big day at the church, and I decided that I was going to get the van and take it to pick up some of my friends from the neighborhood. We drove all throughout the north side of our city in a church van full of gang members smoking weed.

I had one last stop before heading back to church to drop the van off when everything changed. I parked the van in a neighborhood and ran to find a friend to join us. Suddenly, I heard a loud bang. People came running up to me telling me the van had crashed into a tree. I had left the keys in the van, and another kid who was with me who didn't know how to drive jumped in the driver's seat. He floored it, and it went right into a tree. I knew we were in trouble now. Adrenaline kicked in, and we tried to get the van out of the tree in hopes that I could return it without being discovered, but it wouldn't move. Then some neighbors came out and called the cops. We all took off running, leaving the van behind and making our way back to our homes. When I got home, I thought I might have gotten away with it. Then there was a knock on my door. It was Nancy. She told me that several people identified me as the driver of the van. I was caught.

CAUGHT

As you can imagine, she was pretty upset that night. She had been advocating and fighting battles on our behalf for a year, and in that moment, we proved all the naysayers right. Our actions showed them we did not belong in the church and that we could not change. At least that's what it felt like from my perspective. From the moment I walked into the church that first day, I felt that people were waiting for me to mess up. And I had finally done it.

I was expelled from the school, kicked out of the program, and at least from my perspective, never wanted to go back to that church ever again. I went back to a public school and back to the gang, sports, and weed. I felt I had messed up more than I could make up for.

I have told countless youth workers I was the type of kid you did not want in your youth group. I was the type of kid who started fights, did drugs at church, got suspended from school, stole the church van, and plenty of other things I have not disclosed for the sake of the length of this story. I was the type of kid who would have been easy to give up on. But God had a different plan.

About a year later, I got a message from my sister that the pastor of the church wanted me to call him. I'll never forget how confused I was when she told me that. Why would he want me to call him? Was I in more trouble? Did something else come out about what we did? Yet there was something in me that ignited, and I knew I needed to call him.

When I finally reached out and talked to him, I was blown away by what he said to me. He told me that God had been speaking to him about me and that it was time for me to come back to church. I thought he surely had the wrong person, but he meant every word. He knew it was time for me to come back, and even though some people in the church may have been done with me, God was not done with me.

It was then that I knew the pastor, Nancy, and God still had hope for me. I began to pray as soon as I got off the phone. I made a very conscious and sober decision that I would go back to church. I was going to do things the right way. I was going to draw a line in the sand and would not look back to the old way. It was at that moment that I felt my faith come alive. I knew I would never be the same and that I had to make some drastic changes in my life.

It was upon this new turn that I began to fall in love with the story of Saul/Paul. Surely, if God could take a man whose reputation was to persecute Christ-followers and use him the way He did, then I knew that God could do the same with my life. All it took, was a radical encounter with God when I was fifteen in Belize, a few people who refused to give up on me even when I gave them every reason to, and the mercy of God to meet me in the moment where I was invited back to church to follow Him with my whole heart and life.

Chapter 3 Reflection Questions

1. Who was your "Nancy"?

    _____

    _____

    _____

    _____

    _____

2. How can you tell more of your story to encourage others in their faith journey?

    _____

    _____

    _____

    _____

    _____

3. How can you see God moving in the lives of your students—even the difficult ones?

    _____

    _____

    _____

    _____

    _____

 Scan the QR code for teaching videos from author Jose Rodriguez.

PART

02

RELATIONSHIPS

Chapter 4

Presence

I woke up at 2:30 a.m. to my phone ringing. The first time, I just let it ring. I have two rules when it comes to phone calls. One, do not call me after 10 p.m. unless it is an emergency. I define emergencies as being on your way to the hospital or the cops being on their way to your house. The second rule is that you have to call me twice. I intentionally ignore the first one to weed out non-emergency calls.

The phone rang again. I was barely coherent when I answered. On the other end of the line was a student I had been discipling for a few months. I quickly realized that something serious was happening, and I needed to show up.

He told me some of his neighbors just jumped his mom and the cops were on the way to his house. I could hear the anger in his voice and I could tell that he was on the verge of doing something that he would later regret. While the call was an interruption to my sleep, I was so grateful and honored that he would pick up the phone and reach out to me.

Immediately I got out of my bed, threw on some clothes, and drove to his house. I will never forget the drive over that night. I had so many thoughts going through my head: Would I have to fight? Would I be able to stop him? Would he go to jail? What do you say to someone in that moment? It's going to be alright? Just give it to God? What would Jesus do? I was so confused in my head, so I began to pray as I drove to his apartment complex. It was then the Lord showed me that this kid did not need anything. He did not need an answer, a perfect quote, a message, or even a Scripture passage; he just needed my presence. He needed to know he was not alone. I didn't have the perfect answers, but that was not why he called me.

That night, we sat in his living room while his mom was at the hospital. He cussed anybody and everybody he could think of. He was so angry; I could see it in his eyes. All he wanted to do was get revenge for his mom. He felt like not doing something made him less of a man at that moment. I sat on his couch, less than comfortable, with no words. I let him pace. I let him cuss. I let him yell. I let him do everything but leave the house to get revenge.

SHOWING UP

That night, I don't know how much of a spiritual impact I made on him. It was not an altar call moment. We did not have a spiritual conversation. All I knew was that night I kept another teenager out of jail. I helped him know there were people in his life who cared about his decisions, and ultimately, I was there.

On multiple occasions, I have had to write a character letter to a judge or stand with a student while they faced the pain of their own decisions. I can tell you multiple stories just like this one in which the most spiritual thing I could do for a student who was drowning in a world of hurt, anger, fear, and hostility was simply be there for them. In each case, there was not much I could do. There was not much I could say. I couldn't change a judge's mind. I couldn't convince the student to do something better or that it would work out the way they wanted. All I could do was simply be present.

I realize that my journey in urban youth ministry may not look like your journey as a youth worker or youth pastor. No matter what context you are in, God still calls us to be His representatives as the incarnational presence of Jesus to the students we are serving. I know this principle of presence is one of the most powerful things you can learn when working with students who are drowning in a world of trauma. Students do not always want to hear what you say and often couldn't care less about your title, position, church, or faith. What every drowning student needs is somebody to be present to help keep their head above the water.

We have seen this for decades in the inner cities and urban communities around the nation. Students with wild traumatic histories have needed extra support and social and emotional help to stay above water. The impact of trauma is longstanding, shaping beliefs, behaviors, emotions, and even a person's brain over time. Studies on Adverse Childhood Experiences have shown that childhood trauma (including various forms of abuse, neglect, substance abuse, and incarceration in the household) often profoundly shapes physical health, mental health, and relational health for the rest of a student's life—and in many cases, culminates in an early death.[10] Although this has been less robustly researched, we have also observed that trauma can profoundly shape a person's spiritual life and relationship with God as well.

What every drowning student needs is somebody to be present to help keep their head above the water.

As a responsible adult youth worker and somebody who cares about students, you will want to be there as much and as often as you can. The students you are working with, praying for, and even helping now need the presence of a healthy adult who will assist them in seeing life from a different perspective. Changing a student's view on life will rarely come from a deep conversation, though it could. More than likely, it will come from an exposure to the thing you want them to see. For instance, if I want a student to see that healthy marriages exist, I will need to expose them to healthy marriages—not just tell them that healthy marriages exist. If you want a student to see life beyond their current neighborhood or circumstance, take them on a short-term mission trip. They need to be exposed to a different environment than they are experiencing every day.

Your presence in the life of this generation should be the exposure they need to see the life they could live through faith in Jesus Christ. Students are going to see your message way more than they will hear the words you say. The truth is that we are always telling students something. Whether you are talking or not, you are communicating with them in some way. If you don't respond to their text, which I am guilty of occasionally, I am expressing that they are not worth the time to simply respond. I know this sounds harsh, but it is a harsh reality. Students are watching you and how you show up in their lives or not. The idea of showing up is not even limited to being there physically. What about being there emotionally? What about checking on them periodically to see how they are doing with no agenda, no invite to youth group, or no flyer. It is this idea of showing up that makes us present in the lives of our students.

MISSING LINK

I love the local church. I love youth groups and think they are tremendously valuable in the kingdom of God. However, I sometimes struggle with the idea of what success looks like in a local church context. Some settings I have been a part of and witnessed seem crazy successful from the outside. Youth nights are bringing in hundreds of students. They are probably being impacted by the messages and the worship. There is a good chance they can find some level of community among their peers in the group. These are all great things. My conviction is that I feel like we have been experts at asking students to show up for us, for our events, for our church, and have often dropped the ball in showing up for them when it matters.

We know students need community, but that is not all they need. Students need to be taught and shown what it means to be a follower of Jesus.

I have had some incredible opportunities to share the gospel on school campuses all throughout Southern California. I have seen God do some incredible things as I have boldly shared the message of Jesus and students have responded. But in all the calls I have made to follow Christ, the most memorable and impactful moments in my ministry have always been in life-on-life discipleship relationships. I believe that life-on-life discipleship is one of the missing links in American churches.

The issue with discipleship in our churches today is that in many cases we have narrowed it down to just small groups. While I believe in the small group model and have seen tremendous growth in young people through small groups, small groups do not necessarily equal discipleship. They are the equivalent of community, which is an extremely valuable aspect for students—especially now. We know students need community, but that is not all they need. Students need to be taught and shown what it means to be a follower of Jesus.

In some ways, I want to be careful not to overcomplicate the idea of discipleship for students. As somebody who has advocated for discipleship for most of my time in ministry, I have seen a multitude of circumstances where people have struggled to identify what a disciple is and looks like in their

When you boil it all down, Jesus spent three years being present with the disciples and one weekend saving the world.

context. I am sure there are tons of resources out there for how to disciple people in this generation.

We can look throughout the Gospels and find powerful sayings from Jesus. We will discover incredible miracles, and we will find ways Jesus teaches us how to love others. In the Gospels, I think we also see how Jesus modeled the power of presence. Jesus spent all three years of His public ministry with the disciples. That is three years of talks, rebukes, miracles, and being an example of what the life of a believer should look like. When you boil it all down, Jesus spent three years being present with the disciples and one weekend saving the world. I don't say that to be trite. I think it was intentional and integral to Jesus's plan from the start.

When I look at where many ministries put the focus in their church, it's on salvations. It's on the idea of how many people we can see respond to the truth of the gospel. How many people can we give a compelling enough talk to that they put their faith and hope in Jesus? I am saying this as a communicator of the gospel to this generation. I know how important it is to communicate the gospel to people. But I firmly believe there is no convincing from a stage that will outweigh the value of your presence in the life of students who need presence over a message. Your presence is the message.

During the Covid-19 pandemic, we saw the effects of loneliness. In a lot of the work I do on school campuses, one of the biggest complaints we heard when the pandemic first started and schools shut down was that formerly straight-A students were failing. These students were struggling because they needed the presence of people in their lives. Students' anxiety, depression, and suicide rates skyrocketed during the pandemic simply because they were forced to face their issues without the presence of people around them.

I often asked myself why this generation struggled so severely with depression and anxiety before the pandemic hit. A common factor was based on how many students were connected to thousands of people digitally but didn't have anyone to show up for them. A misconception about Gen Z is that they only want to be seen or heard on social media. While thousands of students are making it their goal to go viral, there are also thousands of students who have gone viral drowning in despair. Why is the most connected generation we have ever seen struggling so much in every area of their lives? It's because there is nothing that can replace the power of being present.

Over a dozen times in the Bible, God made the statement, "I am with you." The Creator of heaven and earth knew we needed to be reminded repeatedly that He is with us. I am convinced that this generation needs to be reminded that He is indeed with them as well. Unfortunately, this is a Thomas-like generation. They are a generation that needs to see the nail wounds in His hands to believe that He is resurrected. They are not going to accept only based on what you tell them. Yes, God is with them. However, they are going to need to see it played out in your life by you showing up for them repeatedly.

PRESENCE OVER PROGRAMS

Here is the challenge with the idea of your presence in a young person's life being so powerful: you will find that this responsibility will become mundane. It will be hard at times for you to be excited to show up. It's going to be uncomfortable for your schedule, your time, and your responsibilities. However, it is going to be you showing up for them that will allow the opportunity for you to invite them into your world.

One of the benefits of the pandemic, if you can call it that, was that it forced believers to stop telling people to come to us and find ways and opportunities to go to people. Social media was a big part of that, but the youth groups that I witnessed thrive in the middle of the pandemic were from churches that had a structure and system set up to help leaders be present in the lives of young people. We had to get creative on what that looked like, but it was presence nonetheless. I watched youth groups migrate to Twitch and gaming since so many students were playing video games during the pandemic. This allowed them to remain present in the lives of students. I watched others thoughtfully embrace the TikTok world with hopes of remaining present in the lives of students. I believe that we are going to see things continue to decline. I have read the end of the book and know that things do not get better in the big picture no matter how much we pray or what we do. The one thing that will never change is that we are still called to make disciples.

TRUST ISSUES

Every student needs help. Some of them do not need as much, and to be honest, it's probably a lot easier and much less time-consuming to help those students more. What about the ones who need you to be fully invested for a year before they begin to trust you? These types of teenagers tend to be overwhelmed by the pain of life and have a hard time listening to anybody. They need to see that you will be there in the good times and bad before they will trust you.

Almost every student I have ever worked with had some severe trust issues. They were not the type of students who come to church and believe you just because you say you're a Christian. It takes work, and honestly, most of that work is messy. That messiness might look like responding to calls at two in the morning and only then seeing the walls begin to break down. It's usually not until those walls are broken down that you start to see their lives transform right in front of your eyes. Some students will not even open up to you until they see you are in it for the long haul.

I have worked in a very deliberate way with students on school campuses since 2015. We ask schools to give us up to thirty of their most challenged or at-risk students each semester. When they look around and see thirty students in the same class for the same reason, they have the same suspicion—some adult wants to fix them. It's a recipe for trust issues. The first couple of weeks is always the biggest challenge. We have to work overtime to make sure the students know and understand that we are there *with* them and not just *for* them. It seems like just a tiny change of a word, but there is a vast difference.

Learning all of these lessons took time and some trial and error. When we started, we thought we had the answers and knew how to fix these students. We learned the hard way that the power of presence requires endurance. One young lady stands out clearly in my mind. On the first day of the program, she greeted us by saying she wasn't going to be in this "***** program with these ***** people" and stormed out of the classroom. You can fill in the blanks with your imagination.

That day, I realized if we were going to be effective, we would need to shift our demeanor. We would need to lay down our pride and egos and find a way to show these students we were with them and not against them. That is much easier said than done.

The next week, to our surprise, this young lady came back for the program. However, she was just as irritated as she was the first week. This time, instead of walking out, she decided to take it out on our program director, seeking to pick a fight with him. Thankfully, he was an empathetic, 6'4", ex-college football player, and he gently disarmed her for the day. This proved our shift in perspective and helped us show that we weren't going anywhere and would be there with them for the next ten weeks.

The following week, she came back again. This time, she was not as hostile as she had been the first couple of weeks. Each week, we made it clear to her that her actions or words did not move us and that we still believed in her and would be there with her if she allowed us to be. In the third week, we began to talk about our pain to help students learn to process their pain correctly. As we began to tell our own stories, you could see that she was a lot more disarmed. It was at this point that we began to see a shift in her.

I would love to say that our program and curriculum are so effective and powerful that we see this type of dramatic shift in attitude every time. While I believe in our program, I am

convinced that what helped change this young lady was the presence of our team showing up consistently even when she gave us plenty of reasons not to show up for her.

At the end of our ten weeks with these students, this young lady was like our student ambassador. It was almost as if anything we would talk about, she would affirm in her own colorful way. We began to champion her voice, and she became our biggest ally, advocating for us to her peers. She also became the student who put other students in check when they were doing disrespectful things to us.

When our program ends, we reach out to the administration team from the school to get their feedback. We want the truth. Either the program worked for students or it didn't, and we can live with the results either way. This particular year, we did not see much behavioral, attendance, or grade change in the overall group. It was disheartening until the principal made one statement that changed everything. He made it clear that though we did not see the results we wanted in everybody, we did see results in one person. He said this young lady was the most significant change they had ever seen on their campus. Before our program, she was in the office every week cussing somebody out and causing problems. He said they had not seen her in the office since week three of our program. He said, "If your program did not work for anybody else, I am convinced that it worked for her."

That young lady did not need our curriculum, motivational speeches, or anything else; she needed our presence. She especially needed us to stay close when she was doing her best to push us away.

LIFEGUARDS

While I have never seen someone drown in real life, I have seen people struggle to stay afloat in water. It is usually those moments when they feel they are in the most jeopardy that they kick and scream for somebody to help them. A trained lifeguard knows that to keep somebody from drowning, you get to them and grab them from behind so they are not kicking you and hitting you while you are trying to save them.

There is a chance that you have been committed to helping some young people, and the closer you got, the more they kicked and punched. It's in those moments that I find it hard to stay present. It's difficult when I know the young person is intentionally fighting against my presence. But if we do not commit to being present beyond bad attitudes, arguing, and even blatant disrespect, we never get close enough to help students get to safety.

I want to challenge you to think about the students who have given you the biggest headaches. The ones who have kicked and screamed the loudest. The ones who have fought you tooth and nail to make sure you knew they did not need you or like you. It's those students who require you to be present enough to help them swim to safety.

Would you consider who in your life right now needs to know you are there and you are with them? I am not asking you to be taken advantage of. I am inviting you on a journey to leave the ninety-nine and go after the ones who are fighting you because they are drowning in their own trauma. There is a generation of the ones who need leaders to leave the comfort of the ninety-nine. These students will be the hardest to get through to but the most rewarding in growth and transformation that you know God can do. It will happen through your presence, not just your programs.

Chapter 4 Reflection Questions

1. What are specific ways you can be present in the lives of students who are far from God?

2. How can you shift your ministry from program-heavy to presence-heavy?

3. What can you do to go the extra mile to be present for one student who has been really challenging?

 Scan the QR code for teaching videos from author Jose Rodriguez.

Chapter 5
The Conversation

In a moment, my life began to take a new course. This moment has marked me forever, but it wasn't a conversion moment. It didn't happen in a church service during an altar call or in a profound setting. It happened on a fifty-four-passenger bus in a low-income community after church had been over for more than an hour.

Until this point, my experience at church had been all about the big moments—the altar calls, big events, or the church services that led people to Jesus. It was never about the bus ride. The bus ride was the means to the big moment. Change was not supposed to happen on a school bus for a challenging student like myself, yet it did. Everything changed for me through one conversation on a bus. However, I took the scenic route to get to this conversation.

"DO NOT JUDGE"

Conversations I had most of my childhood revolved around what I couldn't do or accomplish. When your entire upbringing is about not having enough or not being enough, it becomes hard to feel as if you have what it takes to accomplish anything except being what everybody expects you to be. I struggled to think about anything positive.

She had a mission, and it worked—just not in the way you would imagine.

My life felt like a police drama, except my family and I weren't the protagonists. We were the antagonists, drug-infested and on the run. This caused me to have a negative worldview. It was as if my entire life was doomed because of the situation I grew up in. Ultimately, this led me to believe everything about me had to be harmful, and this meant everything about the way I communicated would directly reflect how I viewed myself and my life.

In spite of my upbringing, I knew I was supposed to act differently, but I still chose to behave poorly at church. Every Wednesday night, Nancy would come pick my friends and me up and take us to youth group. We already attended church every Saturday night and eventually on Sunday mornings, but that was not enough. She knew in order to make a difference in our lives, she had to get us out of the neighborhood and the environment we were surrounded by. She had a mission, and it worked—just not in the way you would imagine.

Week after week, we would get on the bus and go directly to the back. Even though we were incredibly loud, we felt like nobody could see or hear us. The number of colorful conversations we had in the back of that bus and being bold enough to taunt other cars and talk about anything and everything we wanted was enough to get my friends and I kicked off the bus. We gave Nancy every reason to ask us to leave.

She was not quiet because she could not hear us. She could hear and see everything we were doing, but she allowed us to be ourselves. She knew our home environments were less than ideal, and we faced a lot before church, so our conversations simply reflected our daily lives. I was used to people seeing and judging me before knowing me. In this case, Nancy knew me but didn't judge me. At this point in my life, I didn't know Matthew 7:1-2: "Do not judge, so that you won't be judged. For you will be judged by the same standard with which you judge others, and you will be measured by the same measure you use." Indeed, it had to be this Scripture that kept Nancy from doing what so many others had done to me before that moment. Instead of judging, Nancy decided to sit and listen, taking the opportunity to learn. What a powerful concept. In a moment that could have been used for something extremely negative, she allowed herself to cast aside her judgments, biases, and even perceptions to learn about the world we lived in. In spite of the opportunities we gave Nancy to be prejudiced or judge us, the life-changing conversation we eventually had on the bus would never have happened if she had done what I expected everybody to do.

FACE YOUR HYPOCRISY

In your time of ministry and leadership, has there ever been a moment when you cast judgment instead of learning? Have you allowed your own biases to dictate how you respond, speak to, or even care for a student? I know I have.

Since all of my ministries have been in urban contexts, I have experienced some pretty crazy and radical stories of pain and trauma. However, I have found that my judgments are usually reserved for church kids or students who seem like they come from well-off or perfect families. This is where I have struggled in ministry to relate, connect, or even get to know students. I have judged that their need is not as bad without even getting to know them.

There are biases in all of us. Whether that's because of race, gender, or socioeconomic status, I think each of us has to be honest about our preconceived notions so we can see beyond the initial impressions. One of the most profound things you can do as a leader is face your hypocrisy. Look for the areas in your life where you preach or teach one thing but have a difficult time living it out. It could be Matthew 22:39, loving your neighbor as yourself, or Matthew 25:40, whatever you do to the least of these you do unto Jesus. It sounds great in the message. It resonates well with those who are listening, but it's much more difficult to live it out in our daily lives. Once we can face and deal with our judgments, we will be empowered to be more effective in lives of the students we find hard to reach.

The hard part about dealing with our judgment is that we tend to excuse in ourselves what we would never excuse in another. We struggle to be brutally honest with ourselves. For example, I expect others to be on time, yet I find myself showing up late to my meetings. We live in a time when people are used to putting filters on everything. In some ways, the filters we put out to others have allowed us to filter our own lives from the truth. We must first confront what we see in the mirror if we dare to reach those God calls us to reach. This is the point of Matthew 7:5. We have to let God take the plank out of our eyes before we can help students take out whatever is in their eyes.

No one wants to display their dirty laundry for the world to see. I'm the same way. But one of the things I am the most committed to during this season of my life is being brutally honest with myself. I would rather embrace the hard truth than lean toward what is more palatable. After all, Scripture makes it clear that the truth sets us free (see John 8:32). Once we all get to a place where we can be honest about our journeys and our prejudices, we can overcome them

> **The hard part about dealing with our judgment is that we tend to excuse in ourselves what we would never excuse in another.**

and make a massive impact on people who do not look like or sound like us.

I love coaching people and helping them in the art of taking internal conversations they have with themselves and making them external. Everybody has an internal discussion based on what you believe about yourself and others. Teachers have internal conversations about students who give them a hard time. The students have internal conversations about the teachers who always give them a hard time. You are having an internal conversation as you read this: *is the material good, and how can I apply it?* I'm sure as you have read up to this point, you have thought of a few students you have known over the years who you could have done more to try and help.

You must be willing to face your internal dialogue so you can see it and change it. Your beliefs dictate your conversations. The same is true for every student you work with. Their conversations are dictated by what they believe. You could be one honest conversation away, with yourself or with a student, from making the most significant impact your ministry has ever seen. One conversation changed the trajectory of my life and set me on a path of dedicating my life to rescuing this generation.

THE COMMON GROUND

In John 4, we see in the Bible what I would consider the closest parallel to my conversation with Nancy. Jesus, a Jew, was on his way to Galilee to escape the murmuring of the Pharisees. He intentionally chose to walk through Samaria, a place and a people the Jews did not associate with. In my context, I often liken these two people groups to rival gangs. These are two groups who are just as passionate about what they believe is right but would not be caught dead seen together, meeting, or talking without being hostile toward each other.

We see this in John 4 when the disciples come back and rejoin Jesus. They knew this conversation was not supposed to be happening but were too afraid to say something to Jesus about it (v. 27). This one conversation could have created an uproar in many ways, yet Jesus still asked for a drink.

The part of this story I think is most impactful for reaching students different from you is not that he talked to the woman from Samaria; it was how He got her to talk back to Him. Sometimes we can overlook that the woman did not have to say a word back to Jesus. She could have just looked at Him and kept on about her regularly scheduled programming. The way Jesus approached this conversation was simply by finding common ground between the two of them.

Walls begin to come down when we find solidarity with those we are trying to reach.

Once he found common ground, Jesus did not demand anything. Instead, He asked the question, "Can I have a drink of water?" The humility we see in this question is what I believe gave the woman the ability and courage to respond to Him. Similarly, demanding things from students we do not know automatically puts us at a disadvantage. Consider the times when we give students simple instructions, like to sit down during service or to lift their hands during worship. To a student who is hard to reach, the fact that you are telling them what to do makes them not want to do it even more. How can we posture our conversation to be full of humility by simply asking the right questions?

Jesus could have begun this conversation with anything. He could have told her about all her failed relationships from the beginning. However, Jesus knew that for her walls to come down and for Him to have the opportunity to connect, He needed to find common ground with this woman. At this moment, the common ground was water. They were both at the well; they were probably both thirsty. Jesus needed water, but she needed water as well. This was the perfect setup for Jesus, the Savior of the world, who lived a sinless and perfect life, to find commonality with a sinful woman who was probably well known for her promiscuity.

Think about that for a second. This is the equivalent of a well-off business owner who has nothing in common with an inner-city kid finding common ground that ultimately breaks the walls down and allows them both to be open to each other. Walls begin to come down when we find solidarity with those we are trying to reach.

You do not have to come from the same background as an at-risk student comes from or talk like they talk or even have the history they have to relate with them. I have worked with youth workers for the past ten years, and one of the things I see the most that keeps them from reaching the least, the last, and the lost, is the idea that they cannot help those students because they have never been through what the students have been through. This very thought can be highly crippling for a ministry.

You may have never been through the level of pain and trauma that some at-risk and high-risk students have gone through. Truthfully, they know that! It's not a secret to anybody. Even with the amount of life that I lived at such an early age, there are students I am currently reaching who make my childhood look like I was at Disneyland every summer. However, you have been through something. There has been some level of disappointment,

I know it may not seem like much, but when you care enough about students to find common ground, you begin to break down their walls so you ultimately earn the right to speak into their lives and potentially share the gospel.

frustration, sin, or pain that you have experienced, right? Of course there is! The most basic place we can identify with every student is pain. I would encourage you to start looking for the places of pain these students have and ask yourself, *where do I have pain also?* Then, find areas where you can stand in solidarity with them. It will make a much more significant impact than any message you will ever preach.

Finding common ground is the best way to break down walls with a student. It does not always have to be something profound like pain. It can be sports, shoes, fashion, TV shows, pop culture, or even a book. The reality is that you have something in common with every student you encounter. The question is, will you work hard enough and stick it out long enough to find what you have in common? To do that, you must first put away your biases, then find common ground.

WHAT DOES SHE KNOW ABOUT BOXING?

Nancy had every right and reason to kick us off the bus for how we acted and everything we did. She could have also told us to stop having those conversations, and she would have been well within her rights. She listened and learned that we were interested in things beyond what we were talking about, and that changed everything for the relationship I had with Nancy.

As I think back to the conversations we had on the back of the bus, I do not ever remember mentioning boxing. I talked a lot about fighting because that is what we did all the time. I don't recall discussing that I liked boxing or that my dad was really into boxing, but somehow, the conversation that changed everything for me started with these words: "So, I hear you like boxing."

Of all the conversations she could have had with me about the Bible, my lifestyle, or my choice of friends, she decided to ask me about boxing. I remember at that moment thinking to myself, *Did she just ask me about boxing?* I was so perplexed.

I imagine I felt the same way the woman at the well felt when Jesus asked her for a drink of water. Of all the things in the world He could have brought up, He chose to ask about water.

My reply was short. "Yes, I do." Then she pressed it further: "Are you watching the Oscar De La Hoya fight coming up?" I thought to myself, *What in the world does she know about Oscar De La Hoya?* Furthermore, how did she know at the time he was mine and my dad's favorite boxer?

The part about bringing up my favorite boxer was probably a coincidence. However, the fact that she asked me about boxing was the furthest from being a coincidence. She knew very little about boxing, but she knew enough to start a conversation. She listened, she learned, and she found common ground.

This one conversation was the moment I credit as the beginning of much of what God has done in my life up to this point. It was a talk about boxing that opened me up to deeper theological conversations. It was a talk about boxing that developed a deeper relationship with Nancy. It was a talk about boxing that would ultimately lead me to the salvation moment in Belize. I know it may not seem like much, but when you care enough about students to find common ground, you begin to break down their walls so you ultimately earn the right to speak into their lives and potentially share the gospel.

Nobody wants to be talked at or talked down to. Students want to be spoken with. I have found that the bigger the wall, the easier it is to break. The problem has been that most people are scared when they see a wall in the first place. Can I take a moment here to encourage you? You have what it takes to break down every barrier that students try to put up. The more the students rebel and push back, the more they need the Holy Spirit in you. It will be your willingness to hang in there and break down walls and barriers that will lead young people to be the first in their families to come to faith. They could be the first in their family to break the cycle of drugs and divorce. They could be the first in their family with a college degree. They could be the first in their family to say yes to the call of God on their life.

I know because I was the first for all of these. A conversation about boxing led me to break the family cycle of drugs, incarceration, and poverty. This same conversation led my entire family to come to believe in the fullness of Jesus's work on the cross! I have seen God lead my whole family to Him because somebody dared not to be moved by my level of rebellion, hate, and anger. She saw beyond the walls I put up, and it changed everything for me. Some students are far from God and need you to see beyond their borders and find common ground. I believe that you can do it.

Father, in the name of Jesus, I pray that you would help me face my own hypocrisy. I pray that you would allow me to see the plank in my eye before I dare try to speak about the speck in a student's eye. Lord, help me to see these students like you saw the woman at the well. Please help me to go the distance even when they push back and rebel. Thank you in advance for the work you are already doing in their lives. Please give me the courage to push past my level of comfort for the sake of these students! In Jesus's name. Amen.

Chapter 5 Reflection Questions

1. What are some of your biases that have kept you from reaching students who have come to your group?

    _____

    _____

    _____

    _____

2. What is God's view of the students who are struggling in your group? What has been your view? How are they the same? How are they different?

    _____

    _____

    _____

    _____

3. What do you have in common with students who are completely different than you?

    _____

    _____

    _____

    _____

 Scan the QR code for teaching videos from author Jose Rodriguez.

RESCUE A GENERATION

Chapter 6
Blending

I will never forget the day I met "Killer." For me, it was a regular Thursday night serving in the bus ministry, going into neighborhoods, picking up students, and bringing them to church. They were from many different schools, neighborhoods, cliques, and even gangs. Each week was challenging, but we saw God do incredible things.

This ministry was so close to my heart—not because I was the pastor or leader but because I used to be one of these students. In fact, a lot of these students had older siblings who knew about who I was before I met Jesus and God radically changed my life. I was very vocal about my story and how I was no longer in a gang and would do anything I possibly could to help students come out of the lifestyle I grew up in. This really did help me to have a level of influence in the lives of these students. I stand by the fact that you do not have to relate in every way to reach students. However, when an entire community sees your transformation, it helps them believe what you are saying.

Everything was going great the night I met "Killer." We arrived at a stop, and I noticed about ten students I didn't know ready to get on the bus. I was immediately excited because this meant we had a chance to meet new students, and hopefully, they would want to connect with our ministry. As each student got on the bus, I asked for their name so I could fill out the attendance sheet. The last young man who got on the bus was about seventeen years old. I asked him what his name was, and his response was, "Killer." I remember thinking to myself, *surely that's not his name, and hopefully, he hasn't earned this name.* Nevertheless, I asked again, trying to figure out his real name. I wanted to know what his mom named him, not what the streets named him. He didn't want to cooperate. At that moment, I had a choice to make. I could let his defiance give him a one-way ticket off the bus, or let him stay. I chose to let him stay. However, I mentally put a target on him.

TARGETING

Using the word *targeting* might seem inappropriate today, considering the turmoil our country has experienced and the role racial profiling has played in it. Let me explain what I mean and how it can help in reaching students who are not complying with what we would like for them to do. What if targeting meant giving special focus to students who are different or not like the others in the group? This could be one of the things that allows you to make a huge impact on young people who are not followers of Christ but are hanging around your ministry.

Let's use my experience with "Killer" as a case study. As he got on the bus, he went to the back where his friends were. I looked back to see if I knew who he was connected with. Fortunately for me, I had a great relationship with some of the students who were friends with "Killer." As the bus started to head back to the church, I asked one of the students who was friends with "Killer" to come see me so I could talk to him for just a minute. My goal was to have him help me keep order on the bus that day. Where I had a relational deficiency with "Killer," I had a great relationship with his friend, and I knew he respected me and my authority on the bus. I asked his friend to help me make sure "Killer" didn't do anything to disrupt the evening.

This is step one in targeting: find someone you both trust who can help bridge a relational gap and serve as a "cooler" for students who might be disruptive or non-compliant. When "Killer" stepped on the bus, I didn't even know his real name and had no common ground with him except the mutual friend we shared. If "Killer" decided to be disruptive that night, I had no relational authority with him to try and stop him. He didn't respect me just because I was a leader in the ministry or a member of the church. When there is a confrontation with students who are non-compliant, it's force versus force, and usually, the strongest force wins. If or when it comes to force versus force with non-compliant students, nobody really wins.

Step two of targeting is to spend time with the student. Once we arrived at church, I made it my priority to get to know "Killer" and to see if he would open up to me. I went to the game room with him and played a video game. I sat next to him during the service and shared a small portion of my story with him. By the end of the night, I had built a great rapport with "Killer."

Thankfully, he gave us no problems. He ended up being respectful to me and the other leaders in the ministry, and on the way home that night, he even told me his name, what school he went to, and a little more about his family life. I put a target on "Killer" that night so that I could try to get to know him in a real and authentic way. In return, I earned his name and information that helped me to stay in contact with him after that night at church.

In every student ministry, there are usually two types of people present. First, there are the students who are excited to be there. Whether or not they love Jesus really is not a factor; some students just love being in a community of people that offers them a safe, fun place. Then there is the other type of students. Like "Killer," they are not there because they want to be. They are usually pressured into coming, either by parents or friends, and they often give a lot of push back for even being there. They often are going to make sure you know they do not want to be there. Those are the students we need to leave the ninety-nine for. Those are the ones who, if we do not put a target on them, get to know them, and love them well while they are there, you may not ever see again. I believe there are students in your youth group who need you to go the extra mile for them. They need you to put a little more effort into getting to know them. Sometimes it's not as much effort as you think. At some point, just for one night, put all your energy into building rapport with this type of student and watch what happens.

BLENDING

If *targeting* is a way to initiate a relationship, then what I call *blending* is a technique to connect and hopefully be heard. Blending is a concept that recognizes the strength of students instead of trying to force your way, opinion, or viewpoint on them. Blending helps students feel valued, in control, and responsible for what they believe and the decisions they make. Blending can work in very aggressive and hostile environments, and it can also work in subtle disagreements.

In Acts 17, the apostle Paul used a blending technique when he engaged in conversation with the people of Athens. He knew these people didn't believe what he believed. Instead of telling them they were wrong or forcing his own viewpoint on them, he found a way to connect with what they already believed. He knew they put a lot of thought and study into their beliefs. If he simply told them what they believed was wrong, it would not only have been arrogant but also demeaning, and, ultimately, unhelpful toward winning their hearts.

Paul leaned into their strengths, and in verse 22, he began to address them by acknowledging their perspective, their intellect, and their view on philosophy. Can you imagine the level of impact we could all have with students who do not agree with us if we would not immediately dismiss their perspectives? That doesn't mean we affirm their beliefs; it means we do as Paul did. As he began to talk about his God, he referenced the statue they worshiped that was inscribed with, "To an unknown God" (Acts 17:23). He didn't immediately tell them to stop worshiping idols. He acknowledged their strengths so he could leverage them later, in hopes of winning their hearts. For as long as I have been alive and in ministry, I have never seen force versus force work out well in any situation. Usually, it causes more problems and chaos for the two opposing parties. The same is true in reaching the least, the last, and the lost.

Can you imagine the level of impact we could all have with students who do not agree with us if we would not immediately dismiss their perspectives?

They are not initially looking for you to tell them what to believe. They need you to acknowledge their strengths and not dismiss them so you can ultimately win their hearts.

"Killer" was not trying to kill anybody at church that night. By refusing to give me his real name, he simply wanted me to know that he was an alpha male and wanted to be in control. The fact that I let him stay in that frame of mind and utilized it to my advantage allowed me to connect with him because I was not meeting force with force. I could have easily told him, "This is my bus, and if you're going to ride it, then I need to know your real name." If I had taken that approach, "Killer" would not have heard the gospel that night. In the post-Christian society we live in, we must be more concerned with winning hearts than arguments. I can win an argument and lose the right to be in a person's life, or I can seek to win their heart even though I lose the initial argument.

BLEND, DON'T COMPROMISE

My fear is that when you learn about a concept like blending, you will think that I am saying you have to lower your standards in order to reach people. Blending is not about lowering standards or compromising our beliefs. It's about lowering judgments, prejudices, and perspectives for the sake of winning the relationship. So often, Christians around the globe are known more for what we hate—sometimes interpreted as *who* we hate—than who we love: Jesus.

There will be moments when you will come in contact at some level with a student who blatantly disagrees with your viewpoint on life, faith, Scriptures, and God. We must learn to not allow our own pride and insecurities to keep us from the ability to reach them. How I approached "Killer" that night did not mean I compromised my values, my integrity, or my faith. It simply meant that I did not allow our initial disagreement to keep me out of a relationship with him.

Our organization does a lot of work on school campuses. When we are on campus, we come in contact with people from every type of background you can imagine. We have had Muslims in our program, students who identify as LGBTQ+, and people who just flat out do not believe what we believe. The moment these students walk into our program, we have a choice to make: we can spend the first day establishing who we are, what we believe, and why we believe it, or we can spend most of our time finding out who they are, what they believe, and why they believe it.

One person in our program who was born a girl has chosen to identify as Todd and wants to be called by masculine pronouns. Todd has been adamant about being called by this name. The school fully supports this decision, and though I disagree with the idea that a person can choose their gender, I am not willing to risk losing the relationship with Todd in the long run. When Todd first came to our program, we could have thumped our Bibles and used our strength to show how wrong this decision is. However, we took the route of hoping maybe we could love Todd in such a way that we would earn the right to have deeper conversations in the future in which we could ask questions about how everything came to this point in Todd's life. Us choosing not to call Todd out at the beginning of our relationship does not compromise what we believe about God, gender, or sin. It simply says that we value Todd as a person more than we disagree with the lifestyle choices Todd has made.

BELONG, THEN BELIEVE

In Mathew 4, Jesus offered two brothers the chance to follow Him. When they answered His call, He told them He would make them fishers of men. This is such a unique passage because it is another example of Jesus blending with people. He saw these men fishing on a boat and didn't tell them to follow just because. He said to follow Him because He could take what they did (fishing) and teach them how to do it for people.

Once the brothers dropped everything in Matthew 4 and followed Jesus, the Bible calls them disciples. Jesus called others to Himself and then began His teaching ministry with them and others. Once we get to Matthew 10, we see Jesus send the disciples out two by two to do ministry themselves for the first time.

As I think about Jesus's model of leadership, it differs from how most churches approach discipleship in America. These guys had no degrees, experience, or certified training. How dare Jesus send them out that quickly and that early when they clearly were not ready yet! I'm being sarcastic, but it hits home for me. When I went on my first mission trip, I was not a believer. I was just doing what I was taught to do. I was taught how to do dramas for the kids in Belize, how to share my "testimony," and to invite kids to follow Jesus. Truthfully, if they did not let me belong before they asked me to believe, I can almost guarantee that I would not be a believer today. On top of that, they didn't just let me belong, they empowered me to do ministry before I was even a believer.

In Matthew 14, we see an example of failure and rescue. The disciples saw Jesus walking on water, and Peter asked to join Him. Jesus allowed him to walk out on the water to Him. Peter had the faith to begin the journey but got distracted and began to sink. Jesus pulled him up from the water and rescued him. In verse 33, those in the boat worshiped Jesus and said He is the Son of God. I'm not trying to split hairs here, but it does not say that Peter made this confession. I think that's important.

Fast forward to Matthew 16. Now we see what we might call a "profession of faith" for Peter. Jesus asked His disciples who they thought He was. Peter responded, "You are the Messiah, the Son of the living God" (Matt. 16:16). This moment came in the last year of Jesus's ministry. This occurred two whole years after Jesus had been spending time with them. I am convinced that we would see many more people come to faith if we would simply allow them to belong, be a part, and participate before we ever ask them to believe.

This is so important because we cannot keep holding people accountable to what *we* believe prior to *them* believing.

The model of Jesus looked like an invitation (see Matthew 4), relationship building and teaching (see Matthew 4-10), empowerment (see Matthew 10), rescue (see Matthew 14), then salvation (Matthew 16). In a lot of Christian circles today, our process for discipleship looks like an invitation to church, altar call and salvation, then discipleship and small groups. Unfortunately, this seems completely opposite from the way Jesus modeled discipleship in the Gospels.

This is such a big deal to me because if I had been expected to follow this pattern, I might not have ever been saved. I was discipled into faith. I was not saved and then discipled (though my discipleship journey has carried on beyond my initial moment of salvation). I believe there are thousands of students in the world who are waiting to belong so they can have a chance to believe. This is the reason we do not push back on calling Todd by that name. As long as we allow Todd to belong and we continue to build a relationship, there will be moments when we can have real, honest conversations about what we believe and hopefully help Todd come to faith in Jesus.

In Matthew 16, right after Peter acknowledged Jesus is Lord, Jesus rebuked him harshly. The first time Jesus gave one of His disciples a stern correction was after Peter identified Him as the Messiah. This is so important because we cannot keep holding people accountable to what *we* believe prior to *them* believing. The moment Peter professed faith in Jesus, he could be held accountable to that commitment. Anything prior to that and Jesus would have been holding Peter accountable to a commitment he had yet to make.

In student ministry today, you are going to find yourself in contact with students who do not believe what you believe. You can allow them to belong without compromising what you believe. If you only want people around you who believe what you believe, my friend, you're not going to be as impactful in ministry as you can be. Make a commitment that you will allow any and every student to belong, even if they do not think how you think, fully participate in your program, and engage with you right away. You have a perfect opportunity to see more Sauls turn to Pauls by engaging and embracing Sauls. That can't and won't happen if you are afraid of their lifestyle, their sin, or their struggles. You can earn the right to introduce these kids to Jesus—it just might take longer.

Winning students' hearts is only going to come on the other side of identifying that they have a tough outer shell. They may not even want to be a part of what you are doing. Those are the students you need to put a target on. Those are the students you need to pursue. As you pursue them, you can use their strengths as an advantage. Blending is a technique that, if used the right way, could potentially help you reach students who are far from God. Make a commitment to look for students like "Killer." Pursue them as if their life depended on it and earn the right to share the gospel with them. You may not reach them all. However, you will reach a lot more by not giving up easily at the first moment of disagreement or disengagement. You have what it takes to go after the least, the last, and the lost. This generation is depending on it.

These principles work when done in a discipleship context. If you are only paying lip service to them but not fully living them out in a close context with students, you won't be as effective as you can be. If we are going to rescue a generation, it's going to happen because we rolled up our sleeves, dove into the water where students were drowning, and committed to getting close enough to them to help. We cannot be afraid of their sin, pain, or trauma. So prepare yourself as we dive into this next section. This might get a little messy. After all, rescuing people was never supposed to be easy. Ask Jesus.

Chapter 6 Reflection Questions

1. Who are the students in your group, neighborhood, or on campuses you can be targeting?

2. In what ways can you blend with a student you have been having a hard time with?

3. What strengths do the students around you have that you can leverage for kingdom impact?

 Scan the QR code for teaching videos from author Jose Rodriguez.

PART

03

F.A.I.L.

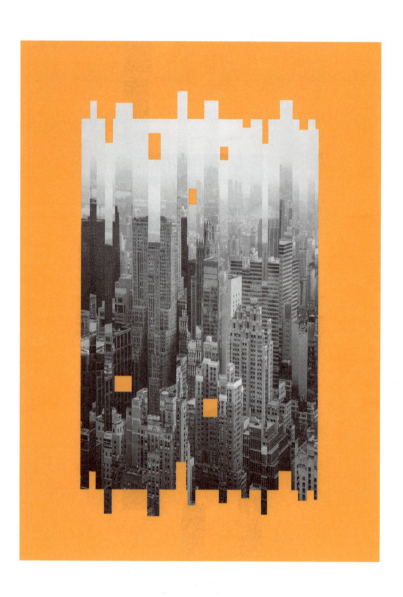

RESCUE A GENERATION

Chapter 7
Faith

"Jose, these students don't need you, they need Jesus."

Ouch! These were painful words to hear. After all, I spent most of my time in ministry going the extra mile to reach students who were far from God. Honestly, I understand the concept theologically, but to believe it in my heart was a little harder for me to do. I realized so much of my ministry had been built upon knowing that Jesus could save lives but not trusting Him to do it. My lack of faith in the full work of the gospel pushed me into working overtime to attempt to save the lives of students when it was never my job in the first place.

Isn't it ironic how quickly we forget what God has done in our lives? My salvation experience alone was miraculous, and that I continued to follow Jesus and live out my faith against all odds was nothing short of the hand of God. However, for some reason, I couldn't grasp that God can and will do the same for "Killer" or any other student I was trying to reach.

As we begin this section about discipling at-risk students, I want to start by challenging your faith in God. I know it may seem like I'm preaching to the choir, but I have been in and around ministry long enough to know that there are moments when we fall into the trap of doing the work, showing up for the ministry, being available for students, and doing a great job accomplishing all that needs to be done, yet we do not fully trust God with the lives of the students He is calling us to reach.

HE DOESN'T NEED YOU

Once I became a follower of Jesus, I was thrown into ministry quickly. The downside of this was that I still had a lot of pain, trauma, and sin to process as I began to lead others. One thing I did early on in ministry was compartmentalize pain, seeking not to be disqualified or allow it to affect my work. Unfortunately, you can only compartmentalize things for so long. At some point, the things you have hidden will come out.

As I was navigating my pain in college, I got into relationships I knew I didn't need to be in. I compromised my integrity and fell into sexual sin. As a result of this, I was placed on a six-month period of leave from the ministry. I remember the devastation of feeling like I could not do the one thing I felt called to do for the rest of my life. I felt even worse about letting my students down.

I was so committed and worked so hard for them because I felt they needed me in their life. At least I thought they did. When my friend told me to relax because they didn't need me, they needed Jesus, it was like a punch to my chest. At the same time, it was an awesome conviction and reminder that the lives of these students were not in my hands but God's hands. Thank God for that! His hands are way bigger than mine.

Sitting out of ministry during those six months was one of the most humbling and powerful things that could have happened to me. It completely shaped my view on ministry. The truth is, you can be the best communicator, at the best church, with the best programs, serving with the best team, and still not see the full possible impact because you don't fully trust God. I learned in those six months that God did not need me, but He wanted me in ministry.

Think about that. At any point, God could raise up and use anybody to do exactly what you are doing and do even better than you. But He chose you—not because He needs you but because He wants you. This takes the pressure off of you having to create a picture-perfect youth ministry with all the Instagram highlights and followers and all the cool swag that awesome ministries are supposed to have. This makes changing the students' lives God's responsibility and faithfulness and obedience our responsibility.

> **He chose you—not because He needs you but because He wants you.**

If you really want to know if you trust God with the work you are doing in ministry, ask yourself this question: are you honoring the Sabbath? I know some of you have the work/life balance thing in the bag and are spending quality rest time. At several points in my ministry, I felt like I had to work seven days a week because God needed me to be "on" every single day. I failed to realize that a part of my having faith in God for the lives of students was me simply honoring the day of rest He commanded I take. I felt as if I couldn't take a rest day because the devil didn't take days off. It was my disobedience to God that showed my lack of trust in Him. What am I going to do on that seventh day that God can't do on the first through the sixth? Absolutely nothing! I'll circle back to this in chapter twelve.

When you think about discipleship, particularly with at-risk students, you must know that it's going to take a lot of commitment, effort, and faithfulness on your part to see students impacted. However, I want you to be sober-minded as we continue this journey together: there will be things that are completely out of your control that you must trust God with. At some point, you will be faced with situations that are painful and hard, and you will not have a solution. You can lean into God's faithfulness in the good and the bad. He is absolutely faithful not just in the altar call, mountaintop experiences. He is just as faithful in the valley of the shadow of death. So a deep, abiding trust in God is the first thing you will need to be effective in ministry in the lives of students who are drowning in a world of trauma. God adds His "super" to our "natural" and multiplies the impact we can make in the life of a person simply by obeying what God has asked us to do. Be faithful to the work you are doing, but trust God with the results.

PROFESSIONAL GOLD DIGGERS

The more I work with students and other youth leaders, the more I realize how important it is not to be moved by a student's initial response to you, to the faith, or to church. There will be some young people who will come and be very excited about Jesus and church one week, only to completely fall away in the next three weeks, never to be seen again. This happens a lot at camp. I love and believe in camps because I have seen so many students impacted by a camp experience. At the same time, I am very honest with students, challenging them not to let the camp experience die out in three weeks. Once students have a camp experience or a powerful moment in church, they tend to be extremely excited about their faith. I believe many students had a genuine experience with God. While they've truly sought to change, their environment and situation did not.

I know that was true for me. I left the mission trip in Belize a completely different person. I made some radical decisions on that trip and I knew I would be different forever—until I got home and realized my family, neighborhood, and school had not changed. Here I was as a fifteen-year-old young man who committed his life to Christ and meant it. I wanted to spend the rest of my life following Jesus, but I was going right back into the pain of my own situation, and I wasn't equipped to handle it. It wasn't long until I slipped back into my old ways.

One of the main responsibilities of youth workers today is to be professional gold diggers. When Jesus first called the disciples to follow Him, they were not the apostles He knew they would one day become. If you look at the life of Peter, there are moments when I would have questioned if he would ever become who God was calling him to become.

Peter in the Gospels gives somebody like me, who was always making mistakes, a lot of hope. He was vocally the most dysfunctional of the disciples. We know Judas betrayed Jesus and stole from the money purse, but we don't see him sticking his foot in his mouth over and over again like we do with Peter. On multiple occasions, we see Peter doing things opposite of the way Jesus wanted him to do them.

Jesus saw beyond Peter's actions and knew what and who he would ultimately become as Jesus continued the journey with him.

Let's journey through the life of Peter in the Gospels and look at the moments where he messed up the most. Jesus, being the greatest youth pastor of all time, had the ability to see beyond Peter's initial sin and issues and see the gold on the inside of him.

In Matthew 14, Peter showed a crazy act of faith: stepping out of the boat and walking on water at Jesus's command. As soon as he noticed the winds and waves, he lost the faith that led him to step out of the boat in the first place. So many times, I have watched students come to faith and naively believe they would never struggle with unbelief again. That is just not the case. As leaders for this generation, we must be properly positioned to be close enough to them when they waver to grab their hand just like Jesus did with Peter. It's dangerous for students to take their eyes off of Jesus and start to sink in their own lives without having a hand to grab.

As Peter's life progressed, we see him confess Jesus as the Messiah (see Matt. 16:16; Mark 8:29). Almost immediately after that conversation, Jesus revealed the suffering He would endure in the days to come. Peter belligerently claimed that would never happen. In that moment, Peter telling the Savior of the world He would never die for humanity took some guts. He was also completely in the wrong, which is why Jesus turned to him and said, "Get behind me, Satan!" (Matt. 16:23). The challenge in this story is not that Jesus rebuked Peter or called him Satan. It's that Jesus was able to see beyond Peter's actions to who Peter was becoming. I have known and currently know so many students who need somebody to see past their moment of acting like Satan to simply believe in who they have the potential to become in the hands of Jesus.

As if being called Satan was not enough, in Matthew 26, as Jesus was being arrested, Peter pulled out a sword and cut a man's ear off. This is the type of thing I could totally see myself doing if I was in the same position. However, Jesus's response to Peter's dysfunction was teaching and healing. He simply put the soldier's ear back on him and told Peter to put his sword away. In other words: "You don't have to fight this battle for me."

We have just walked through three different situations where Peter was less than perfect. Yet Jesus still was committed to who Peter was becoming. Jesus saw beyond his actions and knew what and who he would ultimately become as Jesus continued the journey with him. Now we get to the biggest downfall of Peter's life. On the night of Jesus's arrest, Peter denied that he even knew Jesus—three different times! This is the point when a lot of youth workers would have decided that enough is enough. Jesus's response to people's sin, brokenness, and rebellion has always been different than what we would do if we were in that same position.

At the very end of the book of John, Jesus appeared again to Peter. This was a conversation that could lead Peter to go one of two ways for his future. Instead of scolding him for his failure, Jesus asked Peter a simple question: "Do you love me?" (John 21:17). Peter's response was obvious. Of course he loved Jesus. I know hundreds of urban and at-risk students who would respond the same way Peter did to this question. When I was younger, getting kicked out of church and put on ministry leave for mistakes I made, my response to this question was always the same. Yes, of course I love Jesus. Unfortunately, my brokenness and what I believed about myself and others contributed to me making poor decisions. In that moment, Jesus restored Peter, plotting the course for his future. Only a few weeks later, in Acts 2, on the day of Pentecost, we see Peter stand and address the crowd about the movement of God that was happening as the Holy Spirit came upon the believers that day.

I believe our world is filled with students like Peter who need youth workers to see beyond their actions to their potential. If we are constantly in a state of managing sin in the lives of our students, we will fail to see their hearts fully transformed by the gospel. It is not our responsibility to manage a student's actions or decisions. It is our responsibility to extend grace and be a voice of hope despite a student's downfalls. That doesn't mean there aren't consequences for their actions. I benefitted greatly from my time on the bench after my failure. It just means grace and hope can always be found when a student owns up to their failure and seeks restoration.

If this generation is going to be rescued from the ocean they are drowning in, it's going to be because somebody somewhere saw beyond their sin to who God is calling them to be. They need professional gold diggers in their lives— somebody who is willing to get close enough to dig through the rubble until they find the purpose, future, and life each of these students is called to live. I know firsthand that it is not always easy to see the best in students when they are showing you the worst. However, at some point in your life, you showed the worst as well. Jesus's response to you is always restoration, hope, and a commitment to who you are becoming.

BELIEF AND BEHAVIOR

Let's close this chapter by talking about why students behave the way they do. Sometimes we lack grace for people's decisions because we don't always understand why they would make those decisions. Why would they get into that relationship? Why would they fall into sin? Why would they hang out with those friends? Why would they steal a church van? Why would they get into that fight? Why would they do all the things that seem to cause more damage than good? It's simple: they behave that way because of what they believe.

Every action, whether good or bad, is determined by some level of belief. There are usually three aspects of belief that control how people act:

1) What they believe about themselves

2) What they believe about others

3) What they believe about the thing they are doing

At its core, every sin is a fundamental disbelief in the full work of the gospel. At some level, we think: *God is not enough for me in this area, therefore, I must go do this on my own.* We lie to hide things, we steal to get things, we experiment with our sexuality because we do not fully believe what the Bible tells us about ourselves.

I want you to think about the student who has given you the hardest time in your group. Maybe they came once and have not been back since, or maybe they come week after week and are always causing drama, are disengaged, and are not cooperating with the way you are doing things. Every single week, they are acting how they act for one of these three reasons. The bottom line is, if you really want to see a student's behavior change, you must first be willing to help them change what they believe. Behavior modification is a temporary fix for a life that will eventually go back to the way it was before unless their belief is changed. Life transformation will always happen based on what a student believes.

Believing in the students who are hardest to reach will ultimately give them a chance to change what they believe.

In the same way a student's belief will dictate their behavior, your belief will dictate yours. You will reveal what you believe about these students based on the way you treat them each day. The way Jesus responded to Peter each time he messed up ultimately contributed to who Peter became. The same is true of you. How you respond to the decisions your students make will contribute to who they have the potential to become or not become. I know that sounds like a lot of pressure, but it's not your job to save a student. It is your job to believe in them even when they give you a thousand and one reasons not to believe. You must have faith that they can absolutely become who God is calling them to be. Then, and only then, will your belief in them dictate your behavior toward them. Believing in the students who are hardest to reach will ultimately give them a chance to change what they believe.

As we close this chapter, I want to invite you to look inside and ask yourself: are there students around you who you do not believe in? As we do an introspective look at who we believe in, it's going to be vital that you are brutally honest with yourself in the questions at the end of this chapter. We can only rescue this generation if we believe in them. Outside of that, I believe that our work with young people can absolutely be in vain if we do not really believe what we are saying we believe. I want you to know that if you are reading this, I believe in you. I might not know you, but the fact that you are here now tells me that you are interested enough in helping students that you're diving into a book like this. That tells me a lot about you. You are so necessary for the advancement of God's kingdom in this generation. I need you to believe in them like I believe in you. Better yet, like Jesus believes in you. Remember, He does not need you, He wants you. He chose you for this work. He is not changing His mind anytime soon. Let's continue this journey of rescuing this generation together!

Chapter 7 Reflection Questions

1. How can you trust God more with the students you are trying to reach?

2. In what ways can you believe in students even when they give you reasons not to?

3. What behaviors have you seen in students that are dictated by their beliefs? What can you do about that?

Scan the QR code for teaching videos from author Jose Rodriguez.

RESCUE A GENERATION

Chapter 8
Authority

We find an amazing story in Luke 7. Jesus had just returned to Capernaum and was met by some Jewish leaders. They had been sent by a Roman centurion because one of his most valuable servants was sick and near death. The Roman centurion heard about the miracles Jesus was doing and sent the Jewish elders to get Him to come heal his servant. The Jewish elders arrived and asked Jesus to come with them, and Jesus agreed. As they got closer, the Roman centurion sent friends to stop Jesus from coming. These friends told them that the centurion was a man under the authority of his superior officers, but he was also a man in authority over those who served under him. He understood authority and knew that if Jesus simply spoke the word, his servant would be healed. Jesus was amazed by this man's faith.

Authority is a powerful concept. It's sometimes hard to describe, but you know it when you are near someone in authority. Authority is often found behind a title, a badge, a position, or even a church. However, it should never be expressed only by title or position. For example, police have authority because of their badge but also because they are supposed to be doing good in the communities they serve. Unfortunately, in many communities, the badge has been a way for some officers to abuse their authority. Not to single out police—the same thing happens in businesses, schools, and yes, even churches. People use titles and positions to wrongly wield authority instead of practicing the correct type of authority that comes with their role, title, or position.

Contrary to popular belief, students in urban communities do not have a problem with authority. They just have a problem with misused and abused authority. One of the major issues concerning working with at-risk students is getting them to listen and respond. Many youth workers have asked themselves, *how do I handle situations when students get rebellious and want to do their own thing?*

The leadership guru John Maxwell wrote about different levels of leadership in his book *Developing the Leader Within*. He explored five stages of leadership that I believe can be equated to authority. It's simple: leaders have authority and should understand it and use it wisely.[11]

TITLES & POSITIONS

In Maxwell's five stages, the lowest level of leadership is *positional* leadership. In positional leadership, you find positional authority. In student ministry, this is the type of authority where it's expected for students to respond to you because you are the youth worker or youth pastor. In previous generations, there was a different level of respect for leaders in the church that transcended cultures and neighborhoods. When I was a student, I know I would be respectful when the bus captain came to my house simply because he was from the church.

However, the moment I got on the church bus and started acting out, I found out he was good at using positional authority. I also learned his authority did not go far past that. So when he wanted me to get off his bus simply because he said so, it was as if he was telling me, "I am the boss; therefore, you must listen to what I am telling you." Unfortunately for him, I did not

> **Positional authority is a good thing when used in the right context and the right way. It becomes a bad thing when used out of context with the expectation that position or title automatically gives authority.**

respond well to people who just told me what to do. I needed him to find another way to communicate instead of using his position and title from the church. As you might recall from chapter three, when he put hands on me to pray for me, I did not respond well.

Positional authority typically will not work well with at-risk, urban students. A lot of these students have already seen way too much abuse of positional authority on social media with police brutality, in their homes with parents who say one thing and do another, and even at church with people who tell them to behave a certain way but do not live it out themselves. Utilizing title and position in the church will work best in the church building or at a church event. However, utilizing it outside of that context will get a much different response.

Positional authority is a good thing when used in the right context and the right way. It becomes a bad thing when used out of context with the expectation that position or title automatically gives authority. If you are a youth pastor in the church who has been leading people well and you go do outreach in the middle of an urban community, I can almost promise your title does not carry as much weight as your care for people will.

Urban students do not have a problem with authority. You can see this in every urban community and city through gangs. Gangs are run by authority. In fact, I believe urban students probably have more respect for authority than those who are not from the same environments. In many cases, the authority of their neighborhoods that has been one of the greatest influences on students. You would never hear about an eleven-year-old showing disrespect to the leader of a gang, because the eleven-year-old knows and understands the gang leader's authority. The truth is that his authority is often not felt because of his title but because of the example he sets in how he leads his gang.

EARNING THE RIGHT TO LEAD

Most people follow positional authority because they are required to. However, people follow *permissioned* authority because they want to. This level of leadership is achieved when people give you permission to lead them. You have done something to earn their willingness to listen and respond to you. Leaders usually enter this level of authority by being a caring person for an extended period of time. If you have gotten to this place in the life of an urban or at-risk student, you have accomplished a lot—especially because they have been lied to and had so many promises broken by so many adults in their lives. This has led many to lose trust and hope in leaders.

The third level of leadership is *productional* authority. This is the type of authority you gain when you start having leaders-in-training serve in the ministry with you. In urban communities, you will see this type of authority in the sports world. Because there is a common goal, coaches can get away with talking to students in ways that would not fly in other areas. If a teacher yelled at a student the same way a football or basketball coach does, the response would be completely different. In fact, if you as a youth worker, pastor, teacher, or leader, yell at a student in the same way a coach does, you will not be very happy with the response. In a lot of the schools we work in, the students are into sports and respond well to the productional authority of coaches. However, when counselors and teachers take the same approach, the student's response is almost always, "Don't talk to me like that!" The exact same authority, in a different context, receives a completely different response.

Level four leadership involves gaining authority through *people development.* This is the authority a person gains because of helping others get better in life. In urban communities, authority can be gained by helping people, but loyalty is achieved from the people developed. I have been the beneficiary of some extremely loyal people, even though they don't follow Jesus, simply because of how I tried to serve and be there for them when they needed me.

Once I got out of the gang life, I tried to stay as far from it as possible so I could get my life on track. I enrolled in Bible college and began to make progress. Eventually, I decided it was time to re-engage with those old friends but from my new outlook on life. I set out to reach as many people like me as possible. One day, my phone rang. It was a young man I grew up with in the gang. Together, we were guilty of committing the same crimes in the same neighborhood.

He was reaching out to me because one of our mutual friends had been going through a lot and had attempted suicide three different times that week. He knew I had changed and he wanted me to come talk to him and pray for him. I was so surprised but grateful that I received this call. I responded with wisdom and took an accountability partner along. I did not want to fall into temptation with drugs or the other things that took place with these friends.

When we arrived at the house, the young man was immediately excited to see me because it had been a long time since we'd seen each other. We began to talk about my new life, my time at Bible college, and my hopes to go to Oral Roberts University and play basketball. We decided to go outside and play basketball for a few minutes, and as we played, I got a chance to hear about the situation that led to his suicide attempts. I shared more of my story and was able to pray for him that day in the middle of the neighborhood basketball court.

My friend did not come to faith that day, but he was encouraged and stopped his suicidal thoughts and attempts. Something shifted in my relationship with that group of guys as a result of that visit. In gang culture, respect is the thing everyone wants. A lot of people in gangs will go to great lengths and do a lot of dumb things for the sake of earning respect. I was no different. A big part of why I fought so much growing up and did the things I did came from trying to earn respect.

That moment, simply by showing up and praying for my friend, I began to get the respect from this group that I had been trying to gain for years. It all happened because I helped somebody. In that moment, I didn't just gain respect, I gained a level of loyalty from them I never thought I would get back. When you leave a gang, it's kind of like a divorce.

As I left the basketball court that day, one of the other guys showed me the respect and loyalty that my presence gained. He told me that if I ever needed them to hurt somebody for me—since I was in the church now and couldn't do that for myself—I could call them, and they would take care of it for me. I know that sounds funny, because of course I would never need or ask them to do that. But the fact that they even offered to help me this way said a lot about the loyalty I just gained from them. Level four authority was achieved on that day simply because I helped them.

BEYOND CHURCH

I want to offer a radical idea for how you can achieve level four authority with students involved in your ministry. It will call you to think beyond church. Priority one will always be helping students grow in their faith. But what if you had the courage to go beyond spiritual things and empowered them for life? How can you help students in school or with college applications?

How about job training? What about trying to teach and empower students to become entrepreneurs in life? What if we embraced the idea that one of our main responsibilities as a leader is to help students become better in life in general and not just in their spiritual lives? This type of help in the lives of urban and at-risk students will change not just their lives, but the lives of those who are connected to them. It goes beyond just giving them a fish to teaching them how to fish for themselves.

LEADERS, NOT FRIENDS

The last and final level of authority in leadership is *pinnacle* authority. This is the level of authority that is gained based on reputation alone. It's when people know who you are, give you respect, and respond to your authority based on your name alone.

This is the type of authority we see in Luke 7. The Roman centurion sent people to get Jesus because of the name of Jesus alone. He had heard about the good works Jesus was doing and knew that if He would come to help, there would be results. It's not crazy that the centurion stopped Jesus before He even arrived at the house. He responded to Jesus this way based on his understanding of authority. He knew that all Jesus had to do was speak and the servant would be healed.

I needed to insert this principle here in the book because if you are really going to be effective in discipleship relationships with urban youth, there are going to be plenty of moments when you will need to walk in the authority that God has given you over their lives. Authority is not something to be taken lightly. It is a responsibility from God to steward and govern the people and lives that God has trusted you with. That authority is a big deal, and God wants you to use that authority in a way that will change the lives of young people who are far from God.

I want to caution you about something important. Students don't need more friends; they need leaders. I can't stress this enough. Young people who have grown up in a world of bondage do not need other friends to tell them how bad their bondage is. They need a Moses—somebody willing to lead them out of the place of brokenness into the place of promise. Students may not have the best friends, but I promise you that most students have a group they consider friends. They do not need you to try to fit that role or position. They need you to be the leader who helps get them out of the world of hurt they are drowning in.

Urban students need leaders who are not afraid to call them out on their mess when they find themselves in situations that they do not need to be in. For you to be effective, you must walk in the authority God has given you with students. They do not need you to hide behind your title; they need you to get into the trenches of life with them and earn the right to be followed by helping them get better in life, not just in church. Then you will have the authority God is calling you to as you develop more students.

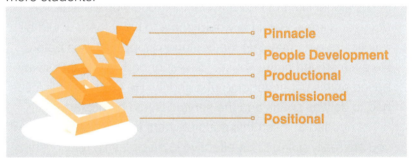

Pinnacle
People Development
Productional
Permissioned
Positional

SPIRITUAL AUTHORITY

Spiritual authority is different from you earning the right to be an authoritative figure in the life of a student. It is given to you by God alone based on the death and resurrection of Jesus. In Matthew, Jesus made it clear that all authority has been given to Him in heaven and on earth (see Matt. 28:18). After saying this, He told His followers to go and make disciples. If Jesus has all authority, and the same power that raised Him from the dead lives in us, that means we have authority over the places God has called us to. You have spiritual authority over every young person God trusts you with, and you get to be the intercessor on their behalf. 1 Timothy 2:1 says that we should be praying, petitioning, and interceding for all people. Your responsibility as a leader to young people must go beyond what you can do in the "natural." We must find time to stand in the gap, intercede for students, and let God move through the supernatural—especially for those who are living in a world of pain and trauma.

While I can't prove this, I am convinced that a big part of how I am living now is because Nancy was not just walking in "natural" authority for me, but leaned on the supernatural. She was exercising her spiritual authority by praying for me every single morning. I believe prayer and intercession work. I believe God responding to Nancy's prayers could have been the only thing keeping me from death, jail, or something that would ruin my life forever.

Earning the right to have authority in the lives of young people could come more from your ability to be a better listener than your ability to lead, your personality, or your ability to speak.

Students who are drowning in a world of pain and trauma need more than for you to just tell them how to live. They need more than self-help books and good messages. They need a person who is willing to cover them in prayer daily. They need God to add the "super" that only comes from prayer combined with the "natural" that comes from discipleship and leadership for them to become all that God is calling them to be. The good news is that prayer works, and He hears our petitions and intercessions. Prayer is a necessary step in committing to reach and rescue the least, the last, and the lost.

DEVELOPING AUTHORITY

Anybody can be a boss. It takes time to become a leader who walks in authority. It will take time for you to develop authority and gain influence with students who are difficult to reach. However, I can tell you from experience that it is time well spent, and there is nothing like being able to share wisdom with a student and see them respond.

One of the ways I developed authority early on in ministry was helping lead the bus ministry on a weekly basis. I was able to be effective in the bus ministry because I spent a lot of time in the neighborhoods where we were inviting students to join us. However, the real secret to me leading at such a high level so early on was the amount of time I spent listening instead of talking.

Week after week, especially in the beginning of my being on a new bus, I would bounce from seat to seat each day just asking questions to the students about life, family, hobbies, music, or sports. I spent very intentional time getting to know the students who were on the bus weekly. That allowed me to break down their walls and build a relationship with them that would ultimately help me lead them as they were coming to church each week. It seemed like the more I listened to them, the more they listened to me.

Earning the right to have authority in the lives of young people could come more from your ability to be a better listener than your ability to lead, your personality, or your ability to speak. It usually took a full month of me building relationships before I would ever stand up at the front of the bus and share my heart, or even instructions, with the group. However, it never failed. When I did start standing up and speaking, I found that students were completely attentive to me simply because I had spent so much time building relationships and earning the right to walk in authority with them.

Over the years, I have been able to talk sternly to students without getting backlash because I placed the relationship over my desire to be heard. Authority without a relationship can be abusive. When people do not know you or your heart and you expect them to listen and respond a certain way, you are contributing to the type of abuse of power that they have seen way too much. We have an amazing opportunity to earn the right to lead this generation. Do not take that lightly. They do not have to listen to you, but they will if you use your authority the right way. I have seen it time and time again.

Chapter 8 Reflection Questions

1. **How can you walk in more authority with students?**

2. **What can you add to your personal devotional life that will help you pray more for students?**

3. **How can you be firmer and loving at the same time with students who are causing problems around you?**

Scan the QR code for teaching videos from author Jose Rodriguez.

RESCUE A GENERATION

Chapter 9
Integrity

It was a normal night at youth group, but I had a plan for something I hoped would be memorable. I wanted to catch my students off guard, so I set the stage like I was about to share the most profound song with the deepest, most moving lyrics that had ever been sung. I played the song. It wasn't by Hillsong or Elevation; it was called *Ju Ju on that Beat.* These were the deeply profound words I wanted my students to hear: "You ugly, you your daddy's son."[12]

My students laughed because this was a song all of them were very familiar with. That night I spoke about looking like your daddy. I wanted to make it clear that each student had to make a choice: who was their daddy, and who would they choose to look like? I gave characteristics of God the Father versus Satan, the father of lies. This combination of surprise, music, and a serious question really connected, and the students were engaged and captured by this message.

I don't share this story to tell you what a great communicator I am. I tell this story because that part of the song truly is profound. Each of us represents our Father in ways we might never realize. The good news is that God gives us the grace to live the life He has called us to live and empowers us through the Holy Spirit to be His sons and daughters. The bad news is that it can feel like a lot of pressure to live under. You mean to tell me that my actions every day of my life are a reflection of my Father? Yes. That is exactly what I am telling you. Your actions privately, publicly, at home, or in front of students represent who your Daddy is.

TWO FATHERS

So who is your father? As a believer, you represent God, your heavenly Father, who is the maker of heaven and earth. He sent Jesus to pay the ultimate price so we could be reconciled to Him as sons and daughters. However, there are still times when we slip back into that old way of thinking and acting and we don't represent God the Father very well. In fact, there are days, if we're all honest with ourselves, when we more resemble the other father. In John 8:44, Jesus referred to the other father, the devil, as the father of lies. Therefore, when we lie, we are not acting like God, our Father, but resembling the devil—the father of lies. I know this sounds pretty basic, but I assure you, it's vitally important.

I have talked to countless students who have extreme levels of pain and trauma at the hands of a lying adult. These lies come in so many forms. They come in the form of promises that were not kept. They also come in the form of lies about people saying they would be there for them forever. I have seen some of the worst lies in a child's life come from moms and dads who lie because they think they are protecting their kid from pain. When a student is lied to, it breaks their trust. It makes them feel like they are not valuable enough for the truth, or even worse, they are not worthy of the truth. This tends to mess up the psyche of a student who needs to trust people for their own well-being.

One of the most impactful lies in my life came from my dad. My dad was in prison on my thirteenth birthday. He was sentenced to three years for a third strike on a driving under the influence charge. I had a conversation on the phone with him on my birthday. He was extremely apologetic that he could not be there. He told me repeatedly that he loved me. Then, at the very end of the phone call, he said something that would stick with me forever. He said, "When I get out, I am going to make up for not being at your birthday." When I got off the phone, I was excited knowing that when my dad got out of prison, I would have another birthday celebration.

A few months after that phone call, my dad was released from prison for good behavior. I am sure he meant everything he said on the phone, but when he got out, he never made up for missing my birthday. I realize now he had a lot of life to catch up on. He needed to get a job and work hard to start providing for the family again. I know this may not sound like a big deal, but I was crushed and clearly have been marked by this broken promise. If the adults in students' lives are lying to them repeatedly, who will be the ones to tell the truth?

TRUTH TELLING

One of the easiest ways for you to build trust among students who are hard to reach is for you to tell the truth. I am not just talking about biblical truth-telling. I assume you already do that. I mean truth-telling about what you say you are going to do. For instance, if you say you are going to pick somebody up at five o'clock, you should tell the truth and be there at five o'clock. That communicates to the students that you are a trustworthy adult, and they will begin to trust you.

This became so clear to me once when I was five minutes late for a meeting with a prominent businessman. When I arrived at the meeting, he told me our meeting was off because I did not respect his time. This hurt and made an impact on me. I connected this to all the times I was late to pick up or meet with a student. What was I communicating to them? I realized my lateness was telling them they were not valuable to me based on me not doing what I said I was going to do when I said I was going to do it. I literally did the same thing my dad did to me because I meant well when I made the promise. I did not intend to break the promise; other things—maybe even more important things—got in the way. The hard part is that students hold on to promises you make, and if you do not come through, then sometimes that genuinely affects their ability to trust, and you become another adult who has lied to them.

VALUE

Most students in urban America are a product of their environment. You can go into any low-income community in the world and see the value of buildings, corner stores, and houses. These things all communicate the value of the location they are in. Run-down communities with beat-up buildings and houses with boarded-up windows communicates to students that this neighborhood is not worth very much.

So many of the students I have worked with over the years have been told nonverbally that they are not worth very much. They have been told through beat-up apartment complexes they live in that they lack value. They have been told through hand-me-down clothes. They have been told through passed-down books to use in school. Urban students tend to get the short end of the stick due to budgets. These things all communicate that they are not very valuable to the world.

Now imagine they come to church. The message from the church is about how valuable they are in the eyes of God—that God sent His Son Jesus to die on the cross for them. They are told that God knows every hair on their heads and that He knew them before they were formed in their mother's womb. These messages all communicate how valuable they are to God.

Here is the challenge: most at-risk and high-risk students have heard and been shown in some way, shape, or form that they are not valuable since childhood. Then they hear the gospel, and they begin to comprehend how valuable they really are. Then a youth worker does not follow through with what he or she promises. Now the student becomes confused because the world has told them they are not valuable, and the church has told them they are, but the youth worker reaffirms through their actions what the world has said.

When we fall into this trap, we have become the very thing that causes students not to trust people. I know Jesus does the saving, but you represent your Father, and you play a role in how they view God. You have a responsibility to treat them with utmost value by respecting their time and keeping promises because to God, they have infinite worth. When our words begin to align with our actions, we can show this generation there is a God who loves them with more than just His words. You get to represent your Father in heaven to an entire generation, and that is a privilege!

PROGRESS, NOT PERFECTION

By the time I came to faith as a teenager, I had already experienced quite a bit of life. So, when I became a follower of Jesus, I had two major challenges:

+ **The first was simply understanding the message of a good God and how much He loved me.** I had a hard time wrapping my mind around Him being a good God who loved me in spite of me.

+ **The second thing I really struggled with was the idea of perfection.** I saw so many people who lived what seemed to be perfect lives. I felt like a complete failure and like I could never live up to that standard. Even the idea of one day being in ministry was so far-fetched—not because I felt God couldn't use me but because I knew how messed up I was. I believed in holiness and living a pure and righteous life. I believed that my soul was saved immediately upon coming to faith and that the process of sanctification would continue to happen until the day I go to be with the Lord. However, what I really struggled with was the idea that for God to use me, I had to be perfect.

Sharing my misconception as a very new believer who came from a worldly point of view might help reveal the struggles of many young people with the same misconceptions in your student ministry. It's so powerful to come to grips with God's grace and how much we need the Holy Spirit to empower us to live the pure and holy lives God is calling us to. When I first came to faith, I found that the more I struggled to live up to the standard, the further it pushed me from trying.

The more time I spent in church, I realized a lot of the people who I thought were living at this untouchable standard were not living at that level at all. Most of them just got good at putting on their Christian mask that painted a picture that their life was perfect. The problem with an urban, at-risk student who grew up in a world of sin, drugs, trauma, and pain seeing people live perfect lives is that they feel like they are too unworthy to even get close to that life.

The truth is, our humanity can help reveal how good God's grace is. As the Lord told the apostle Paul in 2 Corinthians 12:9, "My grace is sufficient for you, for my power is perfected in weakness." The fact that He can take and use a broken, messed up person like me says a lot to other people who struggle as I struggled. I am not saying we should lower God's standards of holiness by any means. I am saying we simply need to be more honest and vocal about our own weaknesses, processes, and struggles so others can see how God helped us overcome. Then they can realize they can overcome just the same.

Early in my ministry, I struggled with thinking that God's love, grace, and mercy was for the perfect families, not for me and my family. I found myself keeping secret sin in my life simply because I felt like nobody else around me struggled the same way I did. Sin is a byproduct of brokenness. The truth is that everybody around me had some level of brokenness they were navigating through; I just had no idea they were just as broken as I was. I thought that because of the messed-up situation I grew up in, my pain, trauma, and sin was worse than everybody else's.

As I continued to serve in ministry, I also began to dive deeper into secret sin. It started with porn, and then it grew into romantic relationships. I didn't start out seeking for the relationships to cross sexual lines, but if you play with fire long enough, you are going to get burned. Ultimately, it all came out, and my secret was exposed. I was disciplined for the first time in ministry. I felt like I let all the teenagers down because I was not the perfect example they needed me to be.

The gospel says to come to Jesus, and He will make you whole. You begin a lifelong process of growing through sanctification.

I was sidelined and told I could not do ministry for six months as I walked through a restoration process. I believe in restoration because the Bible says those who live by the Spirit should gently restore one who falls into sin (see Gal. 6:1). That means somebody should be there to help restore you. I needed help and started to receive healing and therapy so I could process the pain correctly. I realized that in all my lies and secrets, I was actually teaching students a false gospel. I was teaching them that if you came to Jesus, He would make you sinless. That is not the gospel. The gospel says to come to Jesus, and He will make you whole. You begin a lifelong process of growing through sanctification.

When I came back six months later, I was so concerned about how the students would receive me. I was afraid they would not trust me anymore and I would have a hard time getting back into their lives. It was completely the opposite. The students were so gracious and understanding. The grace the students showed me was mind-blowing to me. That is when it hit me: to be effective in reaching urban students, they do not need your perfection, they need your honesty.

SECRET SAUCE

Maybe you already model honesty well. Maybe you have seen it modeled well in leadership. In all my years in church, I have not seen many people model honesty, vulnerability, and grace well. We should seek to do this so we can help people who are struggling with sin. Creating an image that you are living a perfect life is probably making you less effective with your students than you think it is.

One of the things I would say has been my "secret sauce" in ministry, both in church and on campuses, has been my ability to "go there" in conversations. I have become the type of person who is not afraid of being completely honest and vulnerable with my audience. The more I have practiced honesty and vulnerability, the more integrity it has given me with them. I realized people already know I'm not perfect, so the best thing I can do is tell them about my process so they can have hope for themselves to receive grace and mercy.

The reason I am so willing to tell the story of my fall is because I know there are lots of pastors and leaders out there (and maybe even reading this book) who find themselves struggling with sexual sin. Whether it's in the form of porn or an actual relationship, I want you to know there is hope for you to get help and restoration from your sin. The more I tell my story to young people about my fall, the more I see them cry out to God for forgiveness and restoration from their own sin.

I used to think integrity was living a perfect life. I have found integrity is more about living an honest and vulnerable life than it is living a perfect life. People already know you are not perfect. Now you can have the freedom to let them into your process so that they may be healed as well.

HOW MUCH IS TOO MUCH?

I am very aware that some things we face in life should only be told to a spouse, a pastor, or a therapist. There are absolutely things in my life that I do not share with students. Some things are appropriate to share; others aren't. Even when I do share, I don't share all the details. Generalities work just fine. Students don't need the gory details.

I think Jesus models perfectly what to share or not to share when it comes to the things we are facing in our own life. Jesus appeared to the disciples in John 20 after His resurrection from the grave. It was a powerful moment because it proved He had risen from the grave and it wasn't just some fairytale. However, Thomas was not there when Jesus showed up to the party. Thomas was upset and made a very bold statement. He said he would not believe it was Jesus unless he saw Him and touched His wounds with his own hands.

A week later, Jesus appeared to Thomas and offered exactly what Thomas asked of Him. He told Thomas to touch the wounds in His hands and to put his finger in His side (see John 20:27). The Bible says Thomas immediately believed. Isn't it interesting how allowing somebody to touch the broken parts of our lives and stories can cause them to believe in Jesus because of our scars?

Here are just a couple of quick tips on how to share your story as you are navigating your brokenness with students:

1. **Make sure you are not bleeding anymore before you allow them into that space.** If you just got hurt by somebody and you know that wound is still fresh and bleeding, you should not go tell young people about that. You could, however, go tell a counselor or therapist about it. That is the better way to handle that. You must be careful not to bleed out on your students. When Thomas put his finger in Jesus's hands and side, He had the scars, but He was no longer bleeding. Jesus was scarred from the cross and healed enough to allow Thomas into that space. I am not saying you have to be perfect before you tell students about your brokenness. However, I am saying you should make sure you are not still so raw that you contaminate them through what you are sharing.

2. **If you are not bleeding anymore and you have gotten the help you need in those areas in your life, tell the truth about them.** Students do not need you to lie to them as if you have never experienced pain or depression. They would rather you tell the truth and let them know you got help and are continuing to get better in that area. You don't need to share every detail; being general and speaking in broad terms is okay. You also need to remind them, especially when sharing about a struggle with sin, that your struggle does not grant them permission to struggle as well. Encourage them to avoid any pitfalls you may have found along the route of your journey toward Christlikeness.

You do not have to hide your brokenness from students. They need to see that you are not a perfect person and you need the same grace they do. After all, students who are far from God are probably there for a reason. They need somebody like you to be willing to roll up your sleeves and show your scars as you begin to help rescue them from the hopelessness that sin brings into the lives of people. Integrity with students does not mean you are perfect. It means you are honest and vulnerable. This will help students know that Jesus really is a Savior, a healer, and your Lord.

Chapter 9 Reflection Questions

1. **Have you lied to students about something you know you need to repent of?**

2. **In what ways can you be better at keeping your word to your students?**

3. **What do you need to be more honest about in your own life that will help you have more integrity with students?**

 Scan the QR code for teaching videos from author Jose Rodriguez.

RESCUE A GENERATION

Chapter 10
Love

As I've made clear so far in this book, it may take a little more grit and commitment to reach urban students. There is a good chance that because of the brokenness they see all around them, they may not follow Jesus just because you say they should. It's going to take you going the distance for and with them for their hearts to be softened and ultimately for their lives to be changed. That's where love comes in.

Love is common but complex. It is the one thing the Bible says, if done the right way, will never fail. In 1 Corinthians 13, Paul revealed different characteristics of love. I love that this famous description of love comes between two chapters on spiritual gifts. In chapter 12, the apostle Paul wrote about the uniqueness of everyone in the body of Christ and how each person is valuable. In chapter 14, we read about spiritual gifts like prophecy and tongues and the proper application of these gifts. Why would Paul put a chapter on love in this spot? Could it be that he was trying to make the case that love drives both how we serve in the church and use the gifts the Spirit has given us?

Paul made it clear how unique and valuable every believer and their gifts are to the body of Christ. Then in chapter 13, he defined what biblical love really looks like. He is masterful in his description because he covers every aspect of what love should look like as it is lived out in the life of a believer.

> *Love is patient and kind. Love is not jealous or boastful or proud or rude. It does not demand its own way. It is not irritable, and it keeps no record of being wronged. It does not rejoice about injustice but rejoices whenever the truth wins out. Love never gives up, never loses faith, is always hopeful, and endures through every circumstance.*
> —1 Corinthians 13:4-7 (NLT)

Reading this description of love sounds counter-cultural to the type of love we see in our society and sometimes even in our churches. One of the things that used to frustrate me the most when I first came to faith was the way Jesus's love for us was described by Christians. It seemed like a fairy tale. It made me feel like God was on the clouds blowing kisses to me all day simply because He loved me so much.

This became hard for me to reconcile as love because I never saw or felt this type of love growing up. As I dove deeper into the Scriptures myself, I realized this description really doesn't capture the full essence of God's love. The real love described in 1 Corinthians 13 is deeper. It's going to take real love for you to reach and rescue this generation. Real love is not nice, passive, or weak. Real love is furious.

FURIOUS LOVE

As I have worked with some of the toughest students over the years, I have found that it was not the cool, relevant, or cute messages or talks that impacted them the most. It was always the ones that challenged them, called them out, or even got in their faces, that caused them to evaluate the life they were living and make some changes. I'm not telling you to yell at students and then they will get it. I am telling you that it is going to take more than a passive Christianity to rescue students in this generation.

My commitment to going after these young people must outlast my desire for fame, opportunities, and climbing the ministry ladder.

A lot of the students God has allowed me to reach have been students who are straight out of abusive situations, drug-addicted families, and hopelessness. For me to come into their community and tell them about a good God who loves them so much can almost sound like an oxymoron if they do not fully understand what that love looks like.

The one thing that has kept me in the fight over the last fifteen years of urban youth ministry has been furious love. It has been the love of God in me for students. His love has already made my mind up that my commitment to loving and serving these students must be stronger than my emotions. My commitment to going after these young people must outlast my desire for fame, opportunities, and climbing the ministry ladder. I am committed to going the distance for these students so they will know there is a God who loves them.

In 1 Corinthians 1:26, the apostle Paul opened his letter to the church reminding them that not many of them were wise when God called them. Not many of them were talented or well-known when God reached them. However, God takes the foolish things of this world to confound the wise. God is not looking only for the most successful, smartest, or talented students; He is looking for fools. If you want to know if your ministry is being successful in loving furiously, ask yourself how many fools you are reaching. When I say fools, I mean students who might be prone to "acting the fool." When students who cause the most trouble in life experience the fullness of

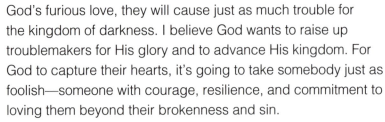

God's furious love, they will cause just as much trouble for the kingdom of darkness. I believe God wants to raise up troublemakers for His glory and to advance His kingdom. For God to capture their hearts, it's going to take somebody just as foolish—someone with courage, resilience, and commitment to loving them beyond their brokenness and sin.

Furious and love are not two words you often hear together. When I learned about God's furious love, it messed up my entire theology. During my time in church, I initially would have promised you that the greatest weapon we have against the enemy is the *power* of God. I'm talking about the kind of power we see all throughout the life of Jesus as He healed the sick and the demon-possessed and turned them into His disciples. However, I have come to believe that the greatest weapon we have against the enemy is not God's power, but God's love.

Students today are extremely broken. They do not need to hear a passive message of faith and encouragement alone. They need to hear that God's love did not just form them but also bled for them. The idea of furious love is not anger directed toward students but being mad at what is keeping them from God's love. It is furious love that will cause you to go the distance with students even when they give you a million reasons not to. It is furious love that will cause you to show up for them when they have already walked out on you. It is furious love that puts you in the position to roll up your sleeves, get out of your comfort zone, and become a rescuer. This generation needs somebody with the furious love of God to dive into the world of hurt that students are drowning in and help rescue them. Love goes the distance, and love never fails!

LOVE AND AUTHORITY

When I was a little kid, I thought my mom loved me because she was nice and my dad did not because he was the disciplinarian in our family. However, my dad taught me a lesson on what love and authority truly look like. It all revolved around the time when I stole the church van (see chapter 3).

I had been lying for several months about my guilt during the investigation. I wasn't going to snitch on anyone, but I wasn't going to confess to any wrongdoing either. I convinced my parents that I was an innocent bystander, and they believed me. Then the detectives called our house and told me they were going to press charges against my friend. As soon as I heard that the charges were not on me, I felt a mixture of relief and conviction. I could not let my friend get in trouble for what I had done. I could have kept quiet and let my friend take the fall, but the conviction was too heavy. I confessed and told my parents I was the one who stole the van.

That was the angriest I had ever seen my dad. Had you been there, you probably would have called Child Protective Services. He had more than a few choice words for me as he paced around the room. Then he got in my face and yelled at me about the path I was taking in life. He asked, "Is this the life you want to live?" Then he balled his fist up and took a swing. I saw my life flash before my eyes. The thing is, he wasn't swinging at me. Instead, he took his anger out on a window. It was then that I knew my dad would never hurt me; he just hated the path my life was on.

My dad's anger was directed at the life I was choosing

to live. It was his love and authority that caused him to leave that day and call the pastor of the church that I stole the van from. He set up a meeting with the pastor, and our family and begged him to drop the charges. To my surprise, the pastor made the decision to drop the charges because he saw my dad plead for my freedom.

My dad did not let me get a pass because the charges were dropped. I was on lockdown for a long time because of the decisions I made. However, watching my dad plead for my life showed me that he loved me more than I ever realized. His love for me that day was not him telling me nice things like he loved me or was proud of me. His love for me that day meant pleading for my future. At the same time, it was his authority and discipline that caused me to think twice about ever wanting to do something like that again.

Love without authority is passive and ineffective. Loving students does not mean you let them do whatever they want whenever they want. Loving students means you correct them. You let them know when they are wrong and how they can get better. Love and authority must go hand and hand.

The Bible makes it clear that God disciplines those He loves (see Heb. 12:6). A part of knowing what love really is means you have experienced correction and discipline. The most important part about rescuing students is learning to find the beautiful balance of love and authority. Love without authority is passive, and authority without love can be abuse.

There are so many students who need the type of love that will plead for their lives, both to people in the world and in prayer. They need love that will not let them get away with anything they want but will love them enough to tell them when they are going down the wrong path. They need the type of love that will fight for them and with them against all the forces of darkness the enemy tries to throw at them.

REAL LOVE

After about a year of being in San Bernardino, there was a young man in my youth group I began to connect with. He seemed like a decent kid but was always getting in trouble at school. As I started to build a relationship with him, it was evident he came from a broken family. His mom tried to be there for him but was always moving around. His dad was on drugs, which was a very toxic situation. I felt this kid had the potential to be special, and I knew God had a big plan for his life, so I had to do my part. He had already experienced so much abuse and trauma by the time I met him that it made it hard for me to really get him to open up and trust me. Nevertheless, I was ready to roll up my sleeves and do whatever it took for me to reach him.

One day, I received a call from the police informing me this young man had run away from home because his dad was trying to hurt him. I was the first person he called. I was saddened by the situation but honored that he called me in his time of need. That meant we were making progress. After an extremely long night and several conversations with law enforcement and Child Protection Services, it was deemed that it was unsafe for him to go back and live with his dad. I didn't realize in that moment I was about to see how far my love for him really went. Sometimes we say we love young people, then it gets awkward or uncomfortable. Our love really comes into question if it means an interruption to our plans or schedule.

Love is not doing for others until they change or because they can change. Love is doing for others so they have an opportunity to change.

As we spoke with the caseworkers, it became clear he did not have any family to go live with. This meant he had two options: he could go to a group home, or he could come live with me on a temporary basis. I had worked in group homes long enough to know it was not the best option for this student, so I opened my home to him.

I would be lying if I said the whole process was easy. It challenged me in every single way that I could be challenged. I knew immediately if I was going to be successful, it was going to be because of God's love and not because of what I could do in my own strength. I needed to press into God's heart for him. We had good days and bad days. We had moments when both of us wanted to quit. There were moments when I asked myself if it was worth doing all of this for somebody who may not ever change. It was that question that taught me the true meaning of love. I heard God ask that same question about me. God has a way of flipping things that humble you and bringing you back to the Father's heart. It was as if He asked me that day if it was worth it to do all that He did for me on the cross if I may never change.

Love is not doing for others until they change or because they can change. Love is doing for others so they have an opportunity to change. Even if they never take the opportunity, the fact that they have one because of love makes all the difference. We love people because God first loved us. While we were yet sinners, God demonstrated His love for us on a cross without any guarantee that we would ever actually change (see Rom. 5:8). Real love is not manipulative or performance-based. Real love is the type of love you can show young people at any point in your ministry. If they never change, would you still love them? If they became worse than they were before you met them, would you still love them?

NO STRINGS ATTACHED

There are days and moments that are so frustrating when you realize some students may never get it. However, I do not want my love for them to be dictated by if they get it or not. I want to love students for who they are, not for who they have the potential to be. What might it look like to love people with no strings attached? What about loving people without an agenda? What about loving people without pushing your expectations on them for what their lives should look like? I fully believe that if we would love people better, our churches would grow more.

People need love. They need people they can count on to be in their corner.

We serve over one thousand students each year on school campuses. We are very honest with the schools we serve that some students will get better, and some will not. We don't promise that a student's behavior is going to change; that's the student's decision, and we can't make it for them. What we do promise the schools and the students is that we will always have their backs. We will always be there for them. We will always believe the best. We absolutely have some powerful stories of change that take place each week on our campuses, but we also have students who spend weeks with us and don't change.

There are young people all around the world who need no-strings-attached love. They need somebody to see them and love them beyond all their brokenness. The more broken they are, the more walls they will put up that you will have to knock down. Real love goes the distance. Real love is the type of love that will spend however much time it takes to break down the walls just so they might be able to experience God's love and change.

I know this generation has been labeled a lot of things. Students are changing so rapidly. Our culture is changing every single day. But the one thing that has always worked in changing someone's life is the one thing that never fails. It will always be real love that goes the distance and gives students a chance to turn their hearts to God. You have a chance to be the one person who loves students who give you every reason not to love them. I pray the prayer of the apostle Paul in Ephesians 3:18: that they would know and understand how long, how wide, how high, and how deep God's love is for them, and I pray they would experience His love through you.

Chapter 10 Reflection Questions

1. How do you define love in your youth group?

2. Have you ever stopped loving a student based on their behavior? How can you love them the way God wants you to love them?

3. What is taking your students out that you can be more furious about and stand against with your students?

Scan the QR code for teaching videos from author Jose Rodriguez.

PART

RESCUED

///

Chapter 11

Safety First

If you have ever been on a flight, you have heard and seen the safety presentation given by the flight attendants. When I first started flying a lot, I was awake and alert for every single safety demonstration and announcement. I wanted to know what I needed to do in case of an emergency. Once I begin to fly quite often, I got the hang of it. It doesn't mean I took it lightly; I just knew what they would say to do if something happened.

In some ways, student ministry is like flying. There are some things we need to know and do to be safe. Right now, picture me standing in the aisle of a plane in one of those little flotation vests and holding up a seat belt, because I'm about to be your flight attendant. Don't zone out and not pay attention. These safety protocols can help you in the event of an emergency and especially as you seek to reach and rescue students in high-risk environments.

TURBULENCE

The worst announcement on a plane is when the pilot tells you before you even take off, "There's going to be some rough air on

> **Student ministry is not like a flight where we know the itinerary and can just buckle up and enjoy the ride.**

this flight." It's a sinking feeling, isn't it? I don't mean to give you that sinking feeling right now, but I'm here to tell you that in reaching the least, last, and lost, there is going to be some rough air. Thankfully, on a plane, there are seatbelts that strap you in when you hit turbulence. Right now, I'm handing you a seatbelt for the turbulence that can occur as you lead in student ministry.

My goal in letting you know there will be turbulence is to prepare you. Just knowing it's going to be tough can help you so that you don't burn out, punk out, or leave easily. I wish every youth worker got instructions that clearly laid out where things will be in five to ten years, but that's just not the case. Student ministry is not like a flight where we know the itinerary and can just buckle up and enjoy the ride. Because our work is so uncertain, many don't make it. So many of our peers leave, quit, or get fired way before their time should be up. I think many of us have lost sight of the impact this makes on students.

Leaving early happens because too many youth workers have not counted the cost prior to getting into a student ministry role. It may have sounded good, felt good, and even looked good on a resume to climb the ladder of church success. When success is the goal, so often, it's easy to abandon the path (and the students) the moment things get difficult or a better opportunity comes along. The rationale is, "surely God wants me to be successful, right?" No. God wants you to be fruitful! He wants you to produce fruit that lasts, and fruit grows in seasons. You must know what season God has you in and prepare to stay for the duration of the season until God releases you.

Youth ministry today is not for the faint of heart. It's going to require you to have thick skin and a soft heart. I know that sounds simple, but it's true. There will be times when your faith will be tested concerning what you believe about God, students, and ministry. It is in those moments that you need to buckle up and weather the turbulence.

There is no easy way to do ministry—especially in a situation where you are trying to reach at-risk students. It is guaranteed that you will encounter some rough air, and your safety in the middle of it all is important. We need you to last in ministry. Your students need you to last in ministry. There is an enemy who would love to take you out prematurely. We cannot let slights, conflict, or offenses ground us from the flight plan the Lord has us on.

DURATION

These are two questions you can ask yourself in each season of ministry that can help you through the turbulence and hang on for the duration:

1) What am I supposed to get out of this season?

2) What am I supposed to give to this season?

As the Lord directs you to the answers to these questions, the answers can help you through the season of ministry, no matter how hard it gets. There are not very many lifetime youth workers who are called to be in vocational youth ministry forever. Can you imagine the impact that could be made in the lives of students and in a community when a youth worker stays for five, ten, or twenty years? I think about the thousands of students who would have known a stable and healthy adult figure in the faith who could have helped them grow into their young adulthood. I think we need youth workers to go the duration not just for themselves or the church but for this generation.

Students need people who will stay in the fight with them even when it gets hard. They need people committed to the journey as they watch students grow. Imagine how powerful it can be when you start with a freshman class and continue with them until they graduate high school and beyond? We know that Jesus was with His disciples for three years. He never said you had to stop after three years. We need youth workers who will move past the discomfort of a season and see students through the duration of their flight.

I echo the apostle Paul's prayer in Philippians 1. He prayed that God, who began a good work in the people of the church at Philippi, would be faithful to complete it. As you are on this journey to reach this generation, I pray that you would find the grace to finish the season you are in well. When seasons are aborted prematurely, students are wounded more than we like to imagine.

Let's be clear: remaining for the duration is not easy. Students have pain and trauma they are dealing with that make our jobs incredibly difficult. Often, we take on student ministry roles right at the time when we are trying to start our own families. To make matters worse, there is often not much money in working with young people—money for our families or our ministry budgets. These challenges, and more, cause many not to last very long in their roles.

That said, there is a right and wrong way to transition. Students can handle people transitioning out of their lives if it's communicated the right way and they are prepared for the change. I also think a transition in a role or church doesn't necessarily mean you must transition the relationship. Just because your season is up in that role does not mean your role is up in the life of a student.

Here's an example of the wrong way to transition: One Wednesday, the student pastor called the pastor of the church and told him he was not coming to youth group that evening because he was quitting. Without warning, suddenly, and out of the blue, he was just gone from the lives of his students. This is an extreme but real example of someone not hanging on for the duration. You might think, *I would never do something like that!* Hopefully you're right, but I personally know the person who did this, and no one knew the pressure he was under and the pain he was navigating. He was right to transition away from his group, but he should have done it a different way.

The youth worker who followed this individual had the challenge of rebuilding trust with the students who were abandoned by their youth pastor. Students are the most affected when we abandon our position in the middle of the flight. You must prepare to remain seated and fasten your seatbelt in the middle of every type of turbulence that you will face.

Students can handle people transitioning out of their lives if it's communicated the right way and they are prepared for the change.

Here's a practical tip to help ease transitions with volunteers in your ministry: Create a clear starting point and a stopping point for when volunteers begin and end their commitment. I call this a season. I ask my volunteers to commit to starting when the season begins and stop when it's over. At the end of each season, I ask each volunteer if they are recommitting for another season. This allows me to help students navigate through transition, which is always important for students who struggle with abandonment and rejection issues. We show students that transition is a part of life, and we can celebrate what God did in the last season and support what He will do in the next. This model also causes people who serve to develop some thick skin because it's not easy to back out unless the end of the season is approaching. As always, there are still going to be people who don't make it the duration, but it limits those and helps create a sustainable culture in ministry. Giving people a start and stop time will help them to endure the whole season and not back out prematurely.

YOUR MASK FIRST

In the flight safety demonstration, at the section on a sudden change in cabin pressure, the flight attendants always say to put your mask on before you help your neighbor with theirs. Every time I hear this, I think about what an important concept this is in ministry. There are going to be moments in ministry—especially serving this generation—when you will find yourself with the wind knocked out of you. It's in those moments when the adrenaline kicks in and you're doing everything you can to help those around you navigate the trauma in their lives that you'll need to check your anger and emotions. We have to make sure we are healthy enough to deal with the pain our students experience. When the cabin pressure changes, your ability to breathe is just as important in that moment as theirs is.

When you think about rescuing a student from dangerous situations, you must have a boldness to walk into that situation and be safe yourself before you can help them. It's so hard to rescue somebody else when you're drowning yourself. For you to be effective at rescuing this generation, you're going to have to take the necessary precautions to make sure you're safe first.

Ministry is hard work. Most people who sign up for it know they will probably be underpaid and under-resourced to fully do their job. In fact, a lot of youth workers are bi-vocational and trying to reach students from the passion God gave them for this generation. When the pressures and demands of life continue to pile up and you are dealing with students' trauma each and every week, you can become unsafe while trying to help other people if you're not prepared. When you get to an unhealthy place, you are at risk of engaging in habits or behaviors that could potentially disqualify you from doing the work you are called to do. Nobody gets into ministry to intentionally get fired, burned out, or placed on leave because of decisions they make. Most decisions that lead to those consequences are simply because at some point along the journey, you forgot to put on your mask first.

We will be most effective in reaching this generation if we practice what we preach. We must create rhythms and routines in our lives that include time with God in prayer, worship, and reading the Bible. We must practice the same things we tell our students to do. We need to model that it works. We've all been guilty of only studying Scriptures as we are preparing for a message. The truth is, we are most effective in ministry when we are doing the things we tell our students to do.

When we try to serve this generation without practicing what we preach, young people are not only going to notice, but they are going to call us out on it. They will see you at some point not doing what you are telling them to do, and they will begin to ask questions about why you can do it and they can't.

One of the toxic things I learned growing up was a saying that my parents used to tell me: "do as I say, not as I do." Unfortunately, that is completely opposite of following Christ. Like Paul says in 1 Corinthians 11, our goal should be to help students do what we do

> **When we try to serve this generation without practicing what we preach, young people are not only going to notice, but they are going to call us out on it.**

and not just what we say. For that to happen, we need to be practitioners of the gospel message. The gospel cannot just be a message that saves them. It needs to be a message that saves us too!

When I publicly fell in ministry, it became clear that I was preaching a message I was not practicing. I would tell students to flee from sexual immorality all while I was battling with it in my own life. Once the carpet was pulled out from under me and everything came to light, it was not only devastating to me, but it was also devastating to the students I was serving. It was another moment that an adult lied to them. However, the good that came from it was the fact that I finally got a chance to take a seat and learn to live and practice the life I taught students to live.

I am not talking about living a perfect life. We know that nobody can live in perfection, but we can all live a devoted life. It took a public fall for God to remind me that I never got into ministry to perform. I got into ministry because of what Jesus did in my life. My fall taught me that I wanted every student in the world to know the God who saved me, forgave me, and restored me. To do that, I needed to get back to my first love.

Sometimes life happens, and it hurts. It is in those moments of pain that we can't just preach through pain, pray about pain, and keep trying to help others through their pain. We must take a moment to get the help we need. We need to put our mask on before we can help somebody else put their mask on. Students need healed people to help them process their own healing. They need people who have been set free to help them be set free from their own pain. They do not need your title, role, or position. They need you to model what health looks like. For some of these students, your marriage will be the only healthy marriage they see. Your life will be the only healthy life they see. And your ministry may be the only ministry they will ever see. I hope that when they look at you, they see someone worth modeling.

Colossians 1:10 says to live a life worthy of your calling. The call of God to reach and rescue young people is a high call. It is an expensive thing to be a part of, and it will cost you a lot. I pray to God that no matter what it costs, you will not sell your soul by trying to help save somebody else's.

EMERGENCY RESPONDERS

Occupational Safety and Health Administration (OSHA) has rules set in place for emergency responders. Their primary goal in setting these rules is simply to protect those who respond to emergencies. If you are going to be a responder to emergencies, you need to be protected. There are laws and protocols that are completely against a person putting themselves in harm's way to help somebody else. As you learn about safety precautions in any job, the main goal is always going to be to ensure your own safety.

Remember, you are not the hero of their story. Know when to say they need a little more professional help than you can offer.

The truth is that this generation is already drowning. They are already in a world of pain and trauma, and you coming in at whatever point in their life does not mean you are going to make a quick turnaround with each of the students you are trying to help. What it does mean is you have a shot to reach and rescue these students. For you to be that person who makes an incredible impact in the lives of young people, it is going to mean you need to hang around in ministry. Students do not just need to see you only preach good messages. They need to see you live good messages over the course of your life. When you find yourself in trouble, go get help.

As I have worked with students who were processing trauma, in some cases, I have realized the pain they were experiencing was over my paygrade. I knew they needed deeper help than I had the ability to give them. Don't get me wrong; I love a good challenge. However, there are certain pains and traumas in the lives of students that I am not qualified to help with. They may need a counselor, therapist, or psychiatrist to get them the proper help that they need.

Remember, you are not the hero of their story. Know when to say they need a little more professional help than you can offer. You are an emergency responder, and your number one priority as you help students is going to be your own health and safety. To make sure that we all make it from one destination to another, we are going to need to be healthy enough to help others when the time is needed.

If you are reading this and are challenged by your own current health, I encourage you to talk to a pastor, Christian counselor, or somebody who can help you get healthy. No one needs you to be a shooting star in ministry. Your students deserve to see you live what you are telling them. Even if you have not been living it, it's not too late for you to get the help you need. A mentor of mine always says you are only as sick as your secrets. Practice James 5:16: confess your sins so that you may be healed, and then you will be more equipped and ready to help students start their own healing process. I fully believe God is more concerned with your soul than He is with your ministry. When we allow God into those broken places in our own lives, He can heal us, and then we can show others how to do the same. I am praying that you have the courage to do whatever it takes to make the call that you may not want to make so that you can get the help you need.

Ministry is hard, but it is also meant to be an enjoyable journey. Even with all the pain, loss, and struggle, ministry has been the most rewarding thing I have ever been a part of. It was never supposed to kill you. It is designed to help you enjoy life more as you help others find faith in Christ. Please enjoy this season. Show students that a life with Christ can be enjoyed!

Chapter 11 Reflection Questions

1. In what ways do you need to recommit to your students for this season?

    _____

    _____

    _____

    _____

    _____

2. What have you been preaching to students that you need to work on more in your own life?

    _____

    _____

    _____

    _____

3. What can you do to make sure you stay healthy as you are rescuing students?

    _____

    _____

    _____

    _____

    _____

 Scan the QR code for teaching videos from author Jose Rodriguez.

Chapter 12
Knowing Your Limits

Growing up, I imagined God like a football coach. He would encourage me when I was having a bad day. He would also tell me to get up and keep pushing every time I fell. This concept of God helped me keep going when things got difficult for me. While it was beneficial for me at that time in my walk with God, it's just not an accurate understanding of His grace.

Grace was always hard for me to define. I've heard it called God's unmerited favor. I've also heard that grace is God's divine ability to do something in and through you that you cannot do on your own. These things are true, but God's grace is so much more.

Grace became very clear to me when I was in college. I often tell students often that I was the least likely person to graduate from college with a bachelor's degree. My entire first year, I was not focused on school and I flunked every class I was enrolled in. It was not because I was not smart enough; I simply lacked the focus and the drive to want to do well. It took a ton of work for me to get back on track, and there were plenty of moments when I wanted to throw in the towel.

> **God's grace does not need my strength or my work to be sufficient. God's grace is perfected when I am at my weakest.**

One day in my junior year, there was a young lady who I was talking to about how God's grace was helping me get through college. I was trying to encourage her to go to college and that God would give her the grace she needed to get there. She did not know that at the time I was on the verge of dropping out. See, I thought God's grace only worked whenever I was working. I thought the harder I tried, the more God would offer His grace to help me. Then I came across 2 Corinthians 12:9. God told the apostle Paul that His grace was all he needed, and His power works best in our weakness. That was when I had a revelation about what real grace is. God's grace does not need my strength or my work to be sufficient. God's grace is perfected when I am at my weakest.

It was at this point that my view of God began to change. Before, I was convinced that every time I was ready to quit, God was like the coaches I have had in the past, yelling at me from the grandstands of heaven to keep on pushing. I felt like the weaker I got, the more God was yelling repeatedly to just keep pushing, try harder, and not give up. After hearing that passage, I began to imagine myself finally lifting up my hands in surrender to Him.

The grace of God has always been waiting on us to stop striving so that we surrender. When I lifted my hands and finally gave up, instead of being frustrated at me like a coach, I feel like God said, "Finally! Now I can step in and do what you could not do in your own strength." This is the reason God's power works best in our weakness. When we are finally at our wit's end, God is at His beginning.

I am more convinced now than ever before that the end of our striving is the beginning of God's grace. As we talk about boundaries in ministry, I want to encourage you that when you get to your breaking point, God doesn't stop just because you do. I think understanding that from the beginning of ministry would have saved me a lot of headaches and heartaches. There were things I thought only I could do when really, God has always been better at coming through than I ever have!

Boundaries in ministry are extremely important if you want to be around for the long term. If your goal is to have a lasting, fruitful ministry, you are going to have to make sure you create structural boundaries for yourself and your students. There is always going to be another emergency, another student who needs you, and another situation happening that you can respond to—especially if you are working in urban areas. It seems as if the enemy never stops trying to wreak havoc on the lives of young people.

SELAH, SABBATH, SABBATICAL

I have established a few boundaries that have helped me over the last fifteen years as I have served students. The first thing I had to do was define an emergency. Everything that feels like an emergency in the moment may not actually be an emergency. There are things students call emergencies that can wait until the morning to be solved. As you probably know, students can be highly emotional. I have had to tell students that an emergency for me is when someone is in danger or the police or other emergency services, like firefighters or Child Protective Services, are involved. When I explain these boundaries, I usually crack the joke, "If she broke up with you, do not call me until the next day."

A big part of my boundaries is the "appropriate time for a call" cut-off. When I was single, it was 10 p.m. That may be too late for some of you, and that time has changed since I have been married. Whatever time you choose, it's important that you choose a time and stick to it. It does not mean that students cannot call you after that time. It just means if they do, it must be an emergency. If you do not clearly define "emergency," a student's bad day could become your emergency, and that's a lot of pressure on you. Remember, when your day ends, God is still at work even when you are not.

One of the other rhythms I wish I would have implemented earlier in my ministry is the rhythm of rest. I was always working on something and did not think I needed to slow down for anything. I now know this was an arrogant position for me to be in and that God honors rest. If you are in ministry now and find yourself tired because of the work you are constantly doing, I want to encourage you that every single day you need a *selah*.

A *selah* is a daily moment when you stop working and breathe. You can spend time with the Father or just decompress. This has become such an important aspect of our ministry at Rescue a Generation that we have a decompression room in our office. Every day, we hear about pain and trauma from students who have endured all kinds of tragedy in their lives, and if we are not careful, we will carry those issues with us every single day. It is vital for our staff to take time throughout their day and *selah* from the noise that is going on all around them. As you become a rescuer, you are going to find the value of *selah* moments in your daily life.

Every day you need a *selah,* and every week you need a Sabbath. Having a Sabbath every single week is not just a good idea, it's a command that God expects us to keep (see Ex. 20:8; Deut. 5:12). That means you need a day when you unplug from ministry and find a way to enjoy the life around you. Go golf, or to the park, or just catch up on some Netflix, but take a complete day off from work—and don't feel bad about it. Remember what

Just because I'm not working doesn't mean God isn't working.

Jesus said in Mark 2:27: "The Sabbath was made for man and not man for the Sabbath."

Finding time to take a day off is not my problem. I struggle with feeling guilty for taking a break. However, coming to a better understanding of God's grace has helped me here. Just because I'm not working doesn't mean God isn't working. Your days off will give you the energy, motivation, and stamina to finish the race God has called you to. Don't feel guilty for taking a day off to rest and recharge; feel convicted if you don't take a day off to rest and recharge.

Every day you need a *selah*, every week you need a Sabbath, and every year you need a sabbatical. If you want to last working with students who are at-risk and high-risk, you are going to need a break for more than a day or two each week. You are going to need a week where you get away—or stay at home—and do whatever you want to do. Spend time with your family, travel around the country, or do a staycation, but make sure you take extended time off. Whatever time your church or ministry offers you for vacation, use every day of it without apology. The issues and challenges you are wrestling with are still going to be there when you get back.

God does not need you to save students. He wants you to partner with Him to save them. That means He is the hero. You are the sidekick. God wants to rescue this generation more than you do. Partnering with Him means you let Him do the work and don't hesitate to develop a healthy rhythm of taking a break, unplugging for the day, and going on vacation.

EMOTIONAL LIMITS

Before you read this section of the book, please be aware that I am about to tell an intense story that you might find troubling. December 2nd, 2015, and April 10th, 2017, were two days I will never forget. Both were days marked by tragedy and darkness and taught me a lot about emotional limits. On both days, I was a first responder to terrible events. The first day was the day of the San Bernardino shooting, which was a terrorist attack where fourteen people died and several others were injured.

I was in a church staff meeting when we saw the news of the shooting. We stopped and prayed for the victims and quickly made the call to get as close as we could so we would be able to minister to our community. We were stopped about half a mile away from the actual site of the shooting. As you can imagine, many people from the community were there, anxious about the well-being of their loved ones. We did not have answers for what was happening, but we knew people needed to know they were not alone, and we were there to help.

Eventually, we were called to gather with other local clergies in a gym where survivors of the attack would be brought and could reunite with their families. When we arrived, we were told our only responsibility was to be there with families as they were waiting for their loved ones to arrive. Several of these families had not heard from their relative since the shooting, so they did not even know if they were safe.

I knew enough by this point in my career not to tell the families that everything was going to be alright because I didn't know if it was or not. I did not know if their loved ones were hurt or killed or what the situation was for each family. So, I just sat and cried with several families.

The buses began arriving about every forty-five minutes. The wait time in between was excruciating for the families. Slowly, one by one, the buses unloaded and families learned if their loved one was safe or not. The reality began to set in for families that their loved one was somehow affected by the shooting. The emotions kicked in and people all over the room began to cry hysterically. It was one of the worst situations I have ever been a part of.

That day, I was running on pure adrenaline for sixteen hours, but I eventually had to go home. The moment I got home,

I felt like all the suppressed emotions from the day came to the surface. I began to weep as I was carrying so much pain from being in that gym with those families.

The next day, we had a lot of work to do as a church. We were planning a prayer vigil for the families, and we knew that people were going to be looking for hope in the middle of the

I learned that on the other side of traumatic situations, your body needs a chance to respond. You cannot just keep on pushing through it; at some point your body will shut down on you.

darkest situation our city had ever faced. However, the next morning when I woke up, it was as if my body wouldn't move. I wasn't paralyzed, I just felt extremely heavy. As I tried to push through and get ready for work, I realized that if I kept pushing, I would not be any good for anybody, including myself. I made the call to take the day off and allow my body to respond to the emotional trauma I had just faced.

The next day my body responded to the rest, and I started to feel better. I was able to get back in the action and help where I was needed. I learned that on the other side of traumatic situations, your body needs a chance to respond. You cannot just keep on pushing through it; at some point, your body will shut down on you.

Two years later, tragedy struck our community again. This time, I was in a staff meeting with Rescue a Generation. We got a call that there had been a shooting in one of the local elementary schools. We were asked to come to a high school where students would be brought to reunite with their families. It was déjà vu as families arrived looking for their children, hoping and praying for their safety.

We did everything we could to serve families and students that day. Ultimately, we stayed on campus until late that night.

At the end of the day, I already knew how my body was going to respond. This time around I had the foresight due to my previous experience not just to take a day off myself but to tell our whole team to take the day off.

When you work in high-intensity situations, you are going to need to make sure you are taking a break as soon as the adrenaline wears off. You do not want to keep on pushing past intense situations because you could end up in a worst-case scenario. We have to know our emotional limits in order to minister to and serve students well.

KNOWING YOUR FIGHT

My hope for you from this chapter is that you will know when to shut it down and come up for air. There is never going to be a shortage of work. The Bible makes it clear that the harvest is plentiful, but the laborers are few (see Matt. 9:37; Luke 10:2). We need more laborers who are around for the marathon that is ministry. We need to see youth workers not just showing up for students but also maintaining their own mental and emotional health. Not every fight will be your fight. You have to have the wisdom to know what your fight is and isn't.

The catalyst that led me to start the Rescue a Generation organization involved the changing of a law in our community. The law allowed school security to give actual tickets to students when they committed small crimes on campus. It was put in place because most of the students' parents would not respond when the school called after a student got in trouble. Law-makers assumed giving a ticket would ensure that parents would respond because now they would have to go to court. Unfortunately, parents still weren't responding, and students would end up with a criminal record that would follow them around for the rest of their lives. It was ineffective and unfair to students and was creating a direct connection to the school-to-prison pipeline.

I mention this process because it was the moment when I realized what my fight was. As much as I was moved by how powerful changing laws could be, I have always known that my impact was going to be directly with students. I witnessed people working on the legal side to change the law and the school and teacher perspective, but I did not see anybody asking to serve the students who were getting in trouble. It was that moment when I

The more I began to understand the details of what our fight was and who we were fighting for, the more I was able to say no to fights that did not include our direct mission.

realized our entire mission would be built around students who are on their way to an unfortunate destination with prison, drugs, gangs, or a life of crime. If we can connect with these students on the early side of them beginning to act this way, then maybe we can play our part in helping to rescue this generation.

The more I began to understand the details of what our fight was and who we were fighting for, the more I was able to say no to fights that did not include our direct mission. Not only have we been able to impact a ton of students, but we are not easily moved from our mission. We know what our fight is and who we are fighting for. Anything else beyond that is a distraction.

If you are a high-capacity leader in youth ministry, there are going to be a ton of opportunities for you to join other causes and fights based on your capacity and talent. This is a good thing, but it can become a bad thing when you do not fully understand your lane and your boundaries. I have chosen to say no to a lot of good ideas if I know it is not my fight. Every opportunity that is presented to you does not have to be your opportunity. Some things you can say no to so you can focus on the things you can directly impact.

Working in youth ministry in any capacity is a full-time job. It takes a lot of hours, commitment, and energy for you to make an impact. Your impact is going to be much larger and much more fruitful if you can go the distance in ministry. That is going to come on the other side of you learning boundaries and when to say no. As a rescuer, there is a time to roll up your sleeves and get in the trenches with students, and there is a time to stay in bed and get some rest. Please value both times because they are just as significant as the other. Just because you are not working doesn't mean God has stopped. He is still at work.

Lord, help my friends who are reading this to learn the boundaries You have called them to live within. I pray that You will help us all understand Your grace and the power of Your strength in our weaknesses. Help us to learn the word no and to say yes to the things You are calling us to. I pray the power of almighty God would strengthen them in their inner being by Your might. In Jesus's name, Amen.

Chapter 12 Reflection Questions

1. What does rest look like to you? How can you add more rest to your daily, weekly, and yearly rhythms?

2. How self-aware are you of your own personal limits? What can you do to grow in your self-awareness?

3. What boundaries do you need to create in order to stay emotionally, mentally, physically, and spiritually healthy?

 Scan the QR code for teaching videos from author Jose Rodriguez.

Chapter 13
Remaining Rescued

Σώζω (sozo) is a Greek word that is translated as "saved" in the Bible. It's a verb that means "to save, keep safe and sound, to rescue from danger or destruction."[13] We know that the goal for this generation is to see them saved. The ultimate agenda for believers is to invite others into the opportunity to be spiritually *sozo'd* and become a disciple of Christ. We know that salvation is the ticket into heaven, but sometimes we make salvation only about a ticket into heaven. When we make salvation only about going to heaven, we miss everything about what our salvation means here on earth.

If salvation was only about going to heaven, then the moment you became saved, there would be no need for you on earth. In fact, at the moment of salvation, what would be best would be to be taken up into heaven like Elijah. Unfortunately, Elijah is one of the few people who have ever been zapped to enter heaven. For the rest of us, we are saved and then left here on earth with a mission to accomplish. The goal for rescuing this generation is not just to get them saved but for them to be on mission for the gospel.

One of the ways we do that is by living a *sozo*'d life. For many people, salvation was a pinnacle moment—the moment that changed everything. For others, like myself, the moment of salvation was powerful, but due to my own brokenness and poor decisions, I needed to be saved more than once. Now don't get nervous—I fully understand that a person is only saved in a spiritual sense one time. I am just saying there were moments when I needed to be saved from my own decisions. There were moments when I needed to be healed from my own continued brokenness. The word *sozo* means more than just a ticket into heaven. It means to be kept safe, rescued, and saved. There are moments beyond your initial decision to follow Christ when you will need Jesus to come rescue you.

What better testimony can you share with a student you are trying to rescue than the testimony that Jesus continues to rescue you? The truth is that God's grace is sufficient not just in the moment of decision but in every moment of failure, frustration, and sin. The number one thing students follow is what you live, not what you say. Your example that God still rescues people will give you much more influence and impact on this generation. To put it another way, your walk will be more impactful than your talk.

Understanding this and living it out allows us to be more vulnerable in our conversations with students. One of the things I tell our team repeatedly is that this generation needs our vulnerability. They need us to show them that it is okay to share how you really feel and that you are processing something in real time. Perfect stories set students up for failure because their stories will not be perfect.

YOU NEED HELP

My pastor has a phrase he uses that describes us all: we are all jacked up. Every person reading this is messed up in some way or another. We are each in our own process of trying to get the help we need in the areas we need it the most. Some hate to admit they are jacked up. You know what that is? Pride. That's jacked up. For others, hearing this and believing it is great news because it means you are not alone in your dysfunction. We don't all have the same issues, but we all have issues.

We have an adversary who is looking for areas of weakness in each of us. He usually does not attack when our guard is up. We see this in Matthew 4 when Jesus went into the wilderness to fast for forty days. The enemy showed up to tempt Him in His most vulnerable state. He approached Jesus at the end of the forty days of fasting when He was weakest and hungriest to try to get Him to give in to temptation.

The enemy uses the same strategy on each of us today. I believe if you have committed your life to rescuing this generation, you have signed up to have a permanent target on your back from the enemy. If we know we have an enemy who tries to attack us when we are weakest, one of the best strategies for protection against him is to be honest about our areas of weakness. It's secrecy that allows him space to wreak havoc on our lives. We must put ourselves in a position to remain rescued as a rescuer.

Every leader needs a leader. Every pastor needs a pastor. Every therapist needs a therapist. Every rescuer needs a rescuer. Who in your life has the power and authority to rescue you? Who do you turn to when things are not going well in your life or marriage? Who knows your weaknesses so that you can get help when your defenses are low? We cannot live out the gospel message if we refuse to participate in it. Each of us needs another person who has access to our lives in the same way we are trying to have access to students' lives.

YOU NEED PEOPLE

One of my concerns with youth workers who are working in high-risk environments is that they become lone rangers and

We have probably all heard the phrase "leadership is lonely." It can be, but it doesn't have to be.

feel like it is them against the world. This mindset can lead to hero syndrome, where we feel like we are the only ones who get it and the only ones who can do the things we do. It's important to know that leaders suffer in isolation and heal in communities. You need people around you who will help you be your most vulnerable and authentic self.

When you have a strong community around you, you will find that it's much easier for you to be vulnerable in front of students because you have a sounding board around you.

The greatest strength of our organization is not my ability to communicate a vision or the programs we have created or our structure. It's our people. I learned this the hard way. For years, I rode the wave of ministry-giftedness but lacked deep, real relationships. I wouldn't allow people into the broken areas in my life. I hid my pain behind the cause of rescuing a generation. I hashtagged and posted about the amazing things God was doing in my life, but nobody knew the pain behind the pictures. I felt like people would disown me if they knew what I was struggling with behind the scenes. I felt people would not be able to handle the real me, so I had to give them a superficial version who appeared to be about His Father's business each and every day. People's perception of me was so important. I needed others to think I had it all together and that I didn't need anybody else.

We have probably all heard the phrase "leadership is lonely." It can be, but it doesn't have to be. Real community is a safe place for you to be honest about who you are and where you are in life. It is a group of people around you who can see you at your worst but still believe in you. I did not think this existed until I had my public fall. It was in that season that God humbled me enough to show me that I needed people desperately. I did not just need people to be excited about my charisma and my ability to do the work; I needed people who would challenge me to be healthier in every aspect of my life. I needed people who I could call when temptation was the strongest to help me overcome my own sinful desires. I needed people who were not going to judge me but embrace me when I needed to be embraced.

In Luke 5, the story of the paralyzed man and his friends perfectly explains what I'm talking about. The friends knew if they could get the paralyzed man to Jesus, he could be healed. They stopped at nothing to get their friend past the crowds to Jesus, even tearing the roof off of a house to lower him right to the feet of the Lord. When Jesus saw the faith of the friends, He forgave the paralyzed man's sins. He clearly saw his outer need for rescue but knew his inner need for forgiveness was greater. Only then did Jesus heal the man's physical condition, telling him to pick up his mat and walk.

Every time I hear this passage, I start thinking about what friends around me I need to get before Jesus. Who in my life is hurting and wounded and in need of a Jesus encounter? Every single time I begin to think about this Scripture, the Holy Spirit reminds me of something important. He doesn't check me because I'm not supposed to help my friends. It is not because there aren't students who are laying on their mats that I need to help carry to Jesus. He checks me because there are multiple characters in that story. It's not always about me being the man who carries others on the mat. Sometimes it's about me having the type of friends who will carry me to Jesus on the mat.

There are moments in our lives when we are the friends doing the carrying

There are moments in our lives when we are the friends doing the carrying and there are moments when we need to be carried.

and there are moments when we need to be carried. What if rescuing a generation wasn't just about what God wants to do in a generation of students but also about the work God wants to do in you? I cannot rescue anyone else if I am drowning in my own sin, trauma, and pain. Before we go out and try to apply these principles to another person, ask yourself: *When was the last time I was rescued? When was the last time I allowed myself to lay on the mat? When is the last time I was not the strong friend trying to carry the weight of every other friend around me?*

If you are having a hard time answering these questions, my friends, you do not need to answer another phone call to help a student. You do not need to speak to another group or prepare another message. You need to allow the hope of the gospel to *sozo* you once again. You need to allow people into your space who can help get you to Jesus when you are having a hard time getting to Him yourself.

The moment we allow the God of heaven to come in and rescue us in every area of our lives is the moment we can embrace our role and responsibility to rescue others. The whole premise of this book is that I can only rescue a generation because I have first been rescued. I can only love a generation because I have first been loved. I can only help to deliver a generation because I have first been delivered. The only thing that qualifies me for this incredibly difficult, challenging, rewarding, fruitful work is the fact that I have been rescued.

YOU NEED THEM

One of the best tools to help you remain rescued is this generation. Let me put it another way: you not only want to rescue this generation, but you need to rescue this generation for you to remain rescued. This may sound confusing, but let me share how this concept has worked in my life.

As I started to become more victorious in my battle with lust, I found myself losing the battle with gluttony. I learned about a weight loss program that fit my needs and schedule perfectly, so I joined it. Immediately, I started losing weight and gaining energy. I lost over thirty pounds in just three months, and people noticed the difference it made in me right away. Because I had success, I was asked to be a coach. At first, I was reluctant because I felt like I couldn't help people lose weight while I was still

This generation doesn't just need me to help rescue them; I need them to help me remain rescued.

overweight. My coach explained it in a way that made it almost impossible for me to say no. He compared it to discipleship. He said, "The power of having people follow you is that it keeps you locked into your own journey for yourself." He challenged me to find a few friends I could lead in the weight loss process. I knew immediately that he was right. If I was going to stay committed to the program, it was going to be because I had other people who were watching me and depending on me. Ultimately, it wasn't just the program that kept me losing the weight; it was the fact that I knew people were watching and following me.

Here's the connection: This generation doesn't just need me to help rescue them; I need them to help me remain rescued. This idea shows up when I'm having some of the hardest conversations with students. It often turns out I need the conversation as much as the student does. The curriculum we developed for our program deals a lot with processing pain. The truth is, every single time we go through the curriculum and have conversations with students, there is an area in my life that the conversation directly applies to.

You need this generation. You need them to anchor you deeper in your own faith walk. You need them to push you into your own healing process. You need them to teach you how to love harder than you ever have. You need them to help you continue to walk in faithfulness with God.

YOU NEED JESUS

Finally, my friends, you need Jesus. I know it may sound cliché and like a church pitch. I am not talking about you needing the Jesus you see on Sunday morning at church only. You need Jesus to fully *sozo* you in every situation. You need Jesus to turn your heart of stone into a heart of flesh. You need Jesus to heal your inner being. You need Jesus to empower you to do all that He has called you to.

There is absolutely no possible way you will live the life God has called you to live and reach the people God has called you to reach without constant desperation for the God who saved you. His salvation for you was not just so you can have a ticket into heaven; it was so you can encounter Him on earth and be transformed by the gospel.

The more I grow in my walk with God, my influence, and my impact, the more I am reminded daily that I am in desperate need of Jesus. He is the vine and I am the branch; apart from Him, I can do nothing (see John 15:5). He is not a lifeline; He is the only lifeline. He is the reason I can do all that I do and the reason I can be the child of God He is calling me to be. In all my years of ministry, I have never needed Him more than I do right now. I am so thankful that He has stepped in repeatedly to rescue me from my own despair. Hopelessness once had a grip on me because of sin and shame, but God has sent His Son Jesus to rescue me. I am a rescuer today because I have first been rescued. You too, friend, can be rescued by Jesus today.

Chapter 13 Reflection Questions

1. What do you need to do to stay in a posture of being healthy and whole as you work with students who are hard to reach?

2. What does your safety net of community look like around you? Do you have one? If not, who could it be?

3. Who do you answer to? Who do you submit your life to? Who pastors you? Who counsels you?

 Scan the QR code for teaching videos from author Jose Rodriguez.

PART

05

CONCLUSION

Chapter 14

Trauma-Informed Discipleship

As we come to the close of the book, I want to spend a little bit of time giving a framework for understanding trauma-informed discipleship. There are reasons at-risk students are considered at-risk. There are reasons why students who do not engage do not engage. There are reasons for defiance and reluctance to be involved, and if we do not understand them, we will find ourselves ineffective and at a disadvantage.

Proverbs 4:7 reveals the supremacy of wisdom and the connection between wisdom and understanding. This book can help you gain knowledge toward reaching and rescuing students, but you cannot just get the knowledge and not seek to understand. In all your getting, get understanding about the students you are trying to reach. Why are they acting the way they are acting? Why are they depressed? Why are they sad and hopeless? If you can find the why, you can then begin to practice the principles.

TRAUMA

According to the Substance Abuse and Mental Health Services Administration, trauma is an event, series of events, or circumstances that are experienced by an individual as physically or emotionally harmful or life-threatening and that has lasting adverse effects on the individual's functioning and mental, physical, emotional, or spiritual well-being.[14]

Trauma is much more prevalent than many recognize, with 70 percent of individuals worldwide having been exposed to some type of traumatic event in their lifetime.[15] However, trauma is even more prevalent in population-dense urban settings. In the US, nearly 90 percent of individuals residing in low-income, urban areas have experienced trauma in their lifetimes, with multiple (rather than single) traumas as normative.[16] Not all trauma is detrimental or repetitive. There are one-time events called acute trauma. Then there is the extreme, complex trauma where an individual is repeatedly hurt by the people they are supposed to depend on for survival. Can you imagine that level of trauma?

What this means is that trauma is a major issue for this generation. This includes factors such as broken families, the pandemic, abuse, neglect, and abandonment, not to mention the brokenness that comes from bad decisions. Trauma is even prevalent in the lives of students who seem well adjusted and are responding well to our ministries. On top of that, not everybody responds to trauma the same way. We need to be informed about trauma so that we know how to respond appropriately and support students as they walk through it. You cannot neglect the pain in their lives if you are trying to help rescue them from hopelessness.

The truth is that we must respond differently to people who have experienced different levels of abuse and pain. We need more empathy so we can sit in the pain of others well and allow them to process their brokenness through the lens of Scripture and the gospel. We cannot over-spiritualize the trauma students have experienced. What I mean by that is spiritually trite and simplistic answer won't do in these situations. We need to know and understand how to respond to students who are hurting.

How does this affect how you approach urban students as opposed to students who may be better off? It must change how we respond and engage them. We do not want to make them feel like

> **Most areas of growth in our lives and in the lives of the students we are trying to reach will come on the other side of being willing to confront, call out, and challenge comfortability in their relationship with God.**

a charity case. People are not projects, they are people. As you embrace urban and at-risk students, you need to value the relationship with the person enough to understand their pain and get to know the person instead of thinking about them as a project for you to help get better.

I am committed to rescuing a generation not because I think they just need to be rescued but because every student I get a chance to help has a name and a story that needs to be told, and they will be influential in reaching other people who have similar backgrounds. People need somebody who is willing to get into the trenches of their brokenness and do life with them.

THE WINNING FORMULA

Now that we have defined trauma, the question that needs to be answered is: what is the formula for success in reaching urban students? That answer is both easy and complex. The easy answer: the gospel. The gospel changes lives. However, the way the gospel has been communicated changes over time. For example, there was a time when hip-hop music was frowned upon in church. Now, if you go to almost any youth group gathering, you are guaranteed to hear some of the latest Christian hip-hop artists communicating the gospel. If you were to ever hear me preach a message, my delivery would be completely different from the way Billy Graham communicated the gospel. The message will never change. Scripture is clear and true, but the method of communicating the truth will always change based on the culture you are living in.

Now the complex answer: it's not just hearing the gospel that makes the difference; it's discipleship that helps develop the heart of any student. Discipleship happens in relationship. Students do not need quick fixes; they need deep relationships. It is virtually impossible for you to be effective in ministry with this generation based on your gifts alone. You need more than your charisma, swag, and shoe game to really see the gospel impact the lives of the students you are working with. You need deep, personal relationships with students.

How do we know if we are doing it well or not? First, I want to be clear that there is not a cookie-cutter way to disciple students. In fact, the closer you get to people, the more of their issues you are going to see and must deal with. The more time you spend with students, the more of your issues they are going to see and must deal with. You need to know ahead of time that if you are doing discipleship well, it's going to get messy.

It's hard to see real transformation without some level of stress, pain, or tension in the process. In fact, most areas of growth in our lives and the lives of the students we are trying to reach will come on the other side of being willing to confront, call out, and challenge comfortability in relationship with God. You cannot get healthy in the gym without having sore muscles. If your discipleship is only fun talks, games, and a few Scriptures, that is not enough to challenge students. I have told students all throughout my ministry that the closer we get, the more of my flaws they will see and the more I am going to challenge the way they live. I give them a choice to decide how close they want to get. I feel like me getting in tense conversations with students about pain, trauma, and life is a sign that they are trusting me enough to allow me into that space. I

Some won't get it, but in others, God will change the trajectory of their entire lives because you committed to being in the trenches with them.

hold that space as sacred so that I do not forfeit the opportunity to grow together. The result of real, close relationships is messy. If you factor in the traumatic situations they have faced and the trust issues they may have, it could get messier than you realize. You must know how to respond to a student's mess.

Obviously, Jesus is the greatest disciple-maker of all time, and even He did not bat a thousand! He had eleven successes and one utter failure. Thinking you will be 100 percent effective in reaching at-risk students is not a reality. There will be ones who get it and there will be ones who do not. I believe in the principles found in this book, but no matter how good the principles are, they don't save lives. It's the relationships you have with students who are struggling that make all the difference. Some won't get it, but for others, God will change the trajectory of their entire lives because you committed to being in the trenches with them.

I was talking to a friend the other day about trauma-informed discipleship. In our conversation, we were talking about the effects trauma has on the lives of people and how we often overlook the effects of trauma on people in the Bible. We often forget they were real people, not just characters in a story. There were plenty of stories of trauma in the Bible that have had a lasting effect on people.

Consider the effects of trauma on the children of Israel after they left Egypt. We often focus on the time it took for them to get to the promised land—it took them forty years to travel what should have taken eleven days. That was obviously because of their rebellion and their disobedience to the instructions God gave Moses. Yes, they absolutely complained, murmured, rebelled, and disobeyed, but what might have been the *why* behind all of this behavior? Could it have been partially due to the trauma they faced in slavery? I think it's not only possible, I think it's likely. I would venture to say getting out of Egypt was probably the easy part. Getting them out of their heads from being enslaved in Egypt was much harder. Their consistent traumatic situation contributed to them not trusting leaders, not trusting the journey, and ultimately not trusting God.

You have to approach urban students with patience. You may be a little frustrated when it takes some students eleven days and it takes others forty years. Maybe those times aren't exact, but you get what I'm trying to say. What you define as success in an at-risk student may be completely different from a student who grew up in church with loving parents and access to so many of the resources urban students have been denied or do not have.

Ultimately, you need to understand why people are acting the way they are acting. Then you will need to get close enough to help them process all they are experiencing. This might mean helping them get the professional help of a counselor or therapist. Once you have done that, the next step for you is to prepare yourself for the journey. This is not a quick-fix gospel. This is not one

This generation needs a Moses who is committed to helping them get to the promised land.

of those situations in which you can just tell kids to take their issues to God—especially when many of these students might blame God for their issues.

They are not being rebellious just to be rebellious. They are not acting out for no reason. They are hurting. It didn't take one day to get into the situation they are in, and it's not going to take only one day to get out. This life of rescuing a generation may literally take years. This generation needs a Moses who is committed to helping them get to the promised land. It's going to take multiple times of you going to the mountain to be with the Father on their behalf. It is going to take you correcting them on multiple occasions because it's going to seem like they just don't care. It is going to take you tearing down their idols and the things they are trying to build that are hurting them.

I know it sounds like a lot and can sometimes seem impossible. However, the work you are doing is necessary. You are making a huge difference in the lives of the students God is calling you to reach. You may not get there tomorrow, but keep praying, keep believing, and keep rescuing. This generation needs you to help them reach their fullest potential and become the people God is calling them to become. As you continue doing the work God has called you to, use the principles found in this book, develop relationships, and prepare for the longevity of rescuing an urban generation. I believe together we can and we will rescue this generation!

Chapter 14 Reflection Questions

1. How has trauma shaped your own life?

2. How big of an impact do you see trauma having in the life of the students you serve?

3. Are you making disciples or converts? What can you do to make more disciples?

 Scan the QR code for teaching videos from author Jose Rodriguez.

Sources

1. Goodstein, Laurie. "Evangelicals Fear the Loss of Their Teenagers." The New York Times. The New York Times, October 6, 2006. https://www.nytimes.com/2006/10/06/us/06evangelical.html

2. Morrow, Jonathan. "Only 4 Percent of Gen Z Have a Biblical Worldview." Impact 360 Institute, May 26, 2020. https://www.impact360institute.org/articles/4-percent-gen-z-biblical-worldview/.

3. Payne, Ruby Ph.D. 1996 "A Framework For Understanding poverty" Fourth Revised Pdition, Highlands, Tx. Aha! Process Inc.

4. Cohen, Philip. "Does Fatherlessness Cause Crime?" Sociological Images: Does Fatherlessness Cause Crime Comments, November 6, 2013. https://thesocietypages.org/socimages/2013/11/06/does-fatherlessness-cause-juvenile-crime/.

5,6. Sotomayor, Tommy. *A Fatherless America*. United States, 2019. SotoFilms.
7. Hughes-Shaw, Mikhayla. "How Fatherlessness Contributes to Juvenile Delinquency." Kids Imprisoned, July 23, 2020. https://kidsimprisoned.news21.com/blog/2020/07/how-fatherlessness-contributes-to-juvenile-delinquency/.

8. Wallace, Jeff; Lenieta Fix. Essay. In Everybody's Urban, p.16. Birmingham, AL: YM360, 2013.

9. "1921 Tulsa Race Massacre." Tulsa Historical Society & Museum, May 11, 2021. https://www.tulsahistory.org/exhibit/1921-tulsa-race-massacre/#flexible-content.

10. Monnat, Shannon M., and Raeven Faye Chandler. Ms. Long Term Physical Health Consequences of Adverse Childhood Experiences. Sociol Q., 2015.

11. Maxwell, John. Developing the Leader Within. Nashville, TN: Thomas Nelson, 2005.

12. Hilfigerrr, Zay and Zayion McCall,. Juju on That Beat (TZ Anthem). 2016.

13. "G4982 - Sōzō - Strong's Greek Lexicon (KJV)." Blue Letter Bible. Accessed May 9, 2022. https://www.blueletterbible.org/lexicon/g4982/kjv/tr/0-1/.

14. Huang, Larke N, Rebecca Flatow, Tenly Biggs, Sara Afayee, Kelley Smith, Thomas Clark, and Mary Blake. Rep. SAMHSA's Concept of Truama and Guidance for a Trauma-Informed Approach. Baltimore, MD, 2014.

15. Benjet, Corina, et al. "The epidemiology of traumatic event exposure worldwide: results from the World Mental Health Survey Consortium." Psychological medicine 46.2 (2016): 327-343.

16. National Center for Children in Poverty. Basic Facts about Low-Income Children Birth to Age 18, October 2008. Available at: http://www.nccp.org/publications/pub_845.html

Notes

Get the most from this resource.

Customize your study time with a guided experience and additional student ministry resources.

"I'm proof that God still rescues people." —Jose Rodriquez, founder and CEO, Rescue a Generation.

No matter where you live or what your student ministry looks like, Jose Rodriquez will inspire you to step outside your comfort zone with real-life stories of how urban youth are being transformed by the gospel, and he'll equip you with the tools you need to genuinely connect with those hard-to-reach students your ministry is missing.

Supplemental videos featuring author Jose Rodriquez available at Lifeway.com/rescueageneration

This book will equip you to coach, mentor, and rescue urban, at-risk, and hard-to-reach students through:

• Key biblical truths

• Biblical application points

• Real-life illustrations and stories

• Practical elements to implement into your ministry

• Reflection questions at the end of each chapter to help you go deeper into the topic

ADDITIONAL RESOURCES

Rescue a Generation (e-book) 14-chapter e-book that teaches how to connect with hard-to-reach students outside your ministry.

Rescue a Generation (videos) 2-3 minute coaching videos featuring author Jose Rodriguez to supplement each chapter of the *Rescue a Generation* book. Available at lifeway.com/rescueageneration